THE ORDINARY WAYS OF GOD

INSIDE THE BOOK OF RUTH

DAVID H. ROSEBERRY

CONTENTS

COPYRIGHT

For my daughter Elizabeth Fox Roseberry.
Ruth was a woman of extraordinary grace, loyalty,
love, dedication, diligence, and beauty.
In other words, she reminds me of you.

INTRODUCTION

The ways of God are ordinary.

Of course, *God* is not ordinary, not at all, but extraordinary in every way we can imagine, and even in ways we cannot. The Bible is replete with magisterial and magnificent passages like, "Heaven declares the Glory of God!" (Psalm 19:1) and "For the earth will be filled with the knowledge of the glory of the Lord as the waters cover the sea." (Habakkuk 2:14) No, our God is a God of wonder and power.

But His ways are sometimes ordinary.

And, of course, that God moves within human affairs at all is a truly extraordinary fact. He is not some impersonal ooze or "Force" all around us. He can and does interfere in human affairs through supernatural means. His ways can be supernatural, and the way He works and moves in our lives can be spectacular and miraculous.

But for the most part, His ways are usually ordinary.

In saying this, I'm pointing to the truth that God tends to operate "behind the scenes" to accomplish His will. He often shapes our lives and guides us forward during our day-to-day living. God's ways are less often like fireworks that light up the sky and more frequently like a fire in a humble hearth. Typically, the ways and works of God take place in our daily routines, choices, interactions, and decisions.

This truth is good news for all of us. It means we do not need frequent "miraculous moments" to convince us that God is real and involved in our lives. Instead, we can see and sense God's presence and direction in our lives' ordinary, daily affairs.

The New Testament Gospels demonstrate this. Jesus performed many miracles across approximately 33 years of His earthly life. Some people saw these fantastic displays of power and were deeply moved, and they believed. Some were so impressed by Jesus' extraordinary ability that they repented. Some people were even afraid, and they also came to believe in Him. However, the four Gospels record only 37 miracles! Each one of these miracles was wonderful, but they did not take up the majority of our Lord's interest, energy, or passion.

DID JESUS DO ONLY MIRACLES?

Consider this: Jesus performed only two miracles in all the time He was in the city of Jerusalem. The Gospel of John tells us that Jesus did many other signs that were not recorded (John 20:30–31), but this proves the point. Some ways of God are extraordinary, but the Gospels are not jammed with one miracle after another. Instead, the Gospels tell us that Jesus walked, talked, encouraged, guided, corrected, challenged, loved, taught, explained, and trained his disciples. Most of the time, Jesus was simply with them as their Lord. He was with His friends, living the ordinary way of God.

We find this same reality in the Old Testament. There are undoubtedly significant miraculous moments like the Exodus, the revelation of the Ten Commandments, and Jonah's survival in the belly of a fish. However, over the 1,500 years of its writing and compilation, there are only 83 recorded miracles. The vast majority of Old Testament stories focus on the day-to-day faithfulness of God and our challenge to be faithful in response. That is the ordinary way of God.

Today, many of us wish that God would perform just one of the New Testament's 37 miracles or one of the Old Testament's 83 miracles. If only one miracle could be seen *and* verified, given the vast reach of the internet, the entire world would come to have faith in God. Or so we imagine.

But the Scriptures ask us to think about God differently than primarily a miracle worker. They invite us to imagine God's presence and activity in our ordinary, day-to-day lives. To ask, seek, and find God in the most common areas of life is the hallmark of being a believer in God and a disciple of Jesus Christ.

THE BOOK OF RUTH

The Book of Ruth perfectly demonstrates this reality. It is a beautiful story of regular people finding their way through life on a day-by-day basis. As they live out their days, they discover the presence of God guiding, correcting, and providing for them along the way.

God is everywhere in The Book of Ruth, but He never appears. He is a constant redeeming force, but He never speaks. God is the director of this fantastic and crucial story in the Bible, but He never forces anything to happen. He does not command, rebuke, or push. In ways both wonderful and ordinary, God simply allows people to make decisions while guiding them with a gentle hand.

Before we begin, I urge you to read the Book of Ruth from the Bible. I have included the four chapters of Ruth from the King James Bible in the back of this book. The language is wonderfully antique and it conveys the ancient and serious quality of the story itself.

The Book of Ruth is only 85 verses long and should only take you 15 or 20 minutes. I have also included a high-altitude summary to help you get the plot lines and timing of the story. Both the King James Version and my short plot summary are at the end of this book.

Once you've read the Book of Ruth, come back to this point in the book, and join me as we discover how ordinary the everyday way of God is.

PROLOGUE

This is a high-level overview of the storyline. The King James Version of The Book of Ruth is in the back of this book

RUTH CHAPTER 1 - THE LAND OF EMPTY

A famine comes to the Land of Judah in the dark days of the Judges. One family leaves the city of Bethlehem and travels over 50 miles east to the "no man's land" of the Moabites—the Israelites' hated and sworn enemy. The family members' names are Elimelech and his wife, Naomi, and their two sons, Chilion and Mahlon. Shortly after they arrive in Moab, Elimelech dies. The two young men marry two women from Moab, Orpah, and Ruth. After ten childless years, both husbands die. The only members left in the family are three women; three widows without hope.

Naomi hears that the famine has lifted back home and that there is food in Judah. She decides to go back. She strongly encourages her daughters-in-law to remain in Moab. She has no hope for their future, much less her own. After some reluctance, Orpah stays in Moab. Ruth, however, makes a lifelong pledge to Naomi to remain by her mother-in-law's side. So Naomi and Ruth travel to Bethlehem and arrive at the start of the spring harvest.

RUTH CHAPTER 2 - THE LAND OF PLENTY

Soon after they arrive in Bethlehem, Ruth goes to glean from the crops behind the harvest workers. There, she draws the attention of Boaz, a man of some stature and owner of the fields. He asks the foreman about the young woman and learns of her and her pledge to Naomi. Boaz is impressed that this young woman would care for her mother-in-law. He makes special provisions for Ruth to be protected while working.

Naomi remembers that Boaz was her late husband's relative and could fulfill the role and duty of a "kinsman-redeemer" to secure their future and provide a future son for the family legacy. (The concept of a kinsman-redeemer will be explained in due course.) Both women are thinking about marriage. Naomi sees the possibility for Ruth's security; Ruth considers the possibility for Naomi's fulfillment.

Naomi tells Ruth to continue to work in Boaz's fields. Ruth continues to glean there until the end of the barley and wheat harvest.

RUTH CHAPTER 3 - RUTH GETS HER WINGS

Naomi learns that Boaz will be working late one night on the threshing floor. She tells Ruth to prepare and then present herself to Boaz. That night, after some harvest celebrations, Boaz lies on his bed, asleep. Ruth quietly comes in to present herself. At midnight, she lies down at the foot of his bed, uncovers his feet, and asks him to spread his cloak over her. This is a highly symbolic gesture; she is proposing marriage.

Boaz is delighted and immediately agrees. The next day at the city gate, some legal issues have to be addressed.

RUTH CHAPTER 4 - BIRTH AND PROMISE

The legal affairs are settled, Boaz redeems the land and, since the widow (Ruth) comes with the land, he marries her. The Lord gives her conception, and she calls the new son Obed. He is the male heir who is needed to carry the line forward with the family.

In time, Obed becomes the father of Jesse and grandfather of David, who in turn becomes the King of Israel and whose descendant, fourteen generations later, will be Jesus Christ. Twelve hundred years later, when the Gospel of Matthew is written, the last verses in Ruth are transcribed into the genealogy of Jesus. Ruth of Moab and Boaz of Judah are listed in the lineage of the Son of God.

~

FOR THE GLORY OF GOD

The Ordinary Ways of God
Inside the Book of Ruth

David H. Roseberry

RMLBooks
Prosper, Texas

OUT OF THE DARKNESS

In the days when the judges ruled . . .
Ruth 1:1

The events described in the Book of Ruth happen during a time of national apostasy, social unrest, and political disorder. Sound familiar? Yet, out of the darkness of a rebellious nation, this story's light shines like a beacon of hope.

The Book of Ruth comes on the heels of the Book of Judges, which chronicles a downward spiral of corrupt government and leadership failures. Judges is the most binge-worthy book in the Old Testament. It contains some of the most appalling episodes of conquest, love, foolishness, sorrow, disappointment, personal tragedy, and erotic betrayal you'll ever read. More than one commentator has nicknamed it "Generation Degeneration."

After chronicling over 300 years' worth of flawed, foolish, and failed leaders, the Book of Judges ends (mercifully) with these telling words: "Everyone did what was right in his own eyes" (Judges 21:25). That's not only a concise summary of the entire book but also a sad epitaph for all of Israel. A statement commonly attributed to G. K. Chesterton has it, "When men choose not to believe in God, they do not thereafter believe in nothing. They then become capable of believing in anything."

The Book of Judges doesn't end; it collapses. And out of the ruins, one question looms: *How can these people be saved?*

Up to this point, the saga of God's people has featured remarkable leaders and cataclysmic events, and God has rescued His people time after time. But as the Book of Judges closes, we wonder how God can turn His people's hearts back toward Himself. Indeed, it will require a miraculous intervention by an extraordinary leader.

ORDINARY PEOPLE

Instead, we find a simple story about ordinary people.

Doubtful about how this dire situation might be turned around, we encounter the story of Ruth. Her book is short and may even seem simplistic. But it packs a wallop. It is a turning point in the Old Testament saga. It moves us from a place of despair and hopelessness to one of hope and promise for the future.

But how? How does this reorientation of our expectations take place?

That is what we are about to discover. The Book of Ruth tells a simple story about a few ordinary people whose daily lives and choices change everything. As so often happens, God ordains ordinary people's day-to-day affairs to redeem their world—and ours. As we will see, this is the ordinary way of our extraordinary God.

Many people today feel that our times and culture are hurtling toward some terrible destination. Our endless divisive political differences end up crippling nations, communities, businesses, schools, churches, and families. Faith in the ability of our once-strong institutions to set things right has declined. Most people do not feel that there is an institution, party, person, or political leader that can bring us out of the spiral.

One of the most powerful lessons from the Book of Ruth is the most simple of all: God will use ordinary people to bring about the change He intends. This is why the Book of Ruth is so excellent. The ancient land of Israel will not be fixed by a reformer or forced by a government. The changes that will ultimately bring everything into the right order will come through the day-to-day lives and decisions of ordinary people being used by our extraordinary God.

This story that begins in dark times will bring light to enlighten the nation. Why? Because a few ordinary people do ordinary things that God will use in extraordinary ways.

~

God can use ordinary people to bring hope in hard times.

~

THINKING MORE ABOUT IT

- Being similar to Ruth's time of social unrest and political discord, where do you see hope in your community, country, and the world?
- When did you do something in your life that you were sure was ordained by God?
- Comment on the last paragraph of this chapter.

2

THE STORY OF RUTH

Like a painting in a gallery, we can appreciate the story of Ruth both up close and from a distance. We will zoom in on the details of this wonderfully rich story, but for the moment, let's stand back and consider the bigger picture. Let's first look at this masterpiece's frame.

Consider the symmetry of the story itself. In the opening lines, we meet a family of four caught in a stressful situation. There is despair. We also see a family of four at the end, but all the tensions have been resolved. There is hope. There is also a balance between the characters. Ruth is a foreigner, a young woman, and a poor widow. Boaz is an Israelite, an older man, and a wealthy landowner. They are opposites, in a way—but in another, they are very much alike. Both Ruth and Boaz show true selflessness, each acting in selfless and loving ways. They are a symmetrical match.

Such craftsmanship in storytelling highlights something beautiful about the Word of God: It is a work of art. God chose men and women (some scholars believe the author of Ruth was a woman) to write the Bible, and He filled them with the Holy Spirit of God's creative power. They did not make things up, but they crafted their stories skillfully. They wrote accounts of actual events with such internal order and intentional artistry that the stories were both popular and memorable. These writers deserve our appreciation, if not our awe.

A HIDDEN TREASURE

Ruth's short story can be hard to find in our Bibles. It is sandwiched between some of the most massive and impressive books of the Old Testament. The seven books before the Book of Ruth and the six books after it are the Old Testament's "power books": Genesis, Exodus, Leviticus, Numbers, Deuteronomy, Joshua, and Judges come before it, and the First and Second Books of Samuel, Kings, and Chronicles are immediately after. These books of Law and history are filled with astonishing miracles, bigger-than-life heroes and villains, and spectacular events that show off God's extraordinary power and glory.

By comparison, the Book of Ruth is small, short, and ordinary. It is devoid of special effects and powerful displays of supernatural signs and wonders. There is not a single observable miracle. No giants arise or sword-fights occur; no battles are won or lost. There are no mysterious pillars of fire or talking fiery bushes. The Book of Ruth has none of that. Instead, it has ordinary people surviving in the ways ordinary people do. There are only eight named persons in the story—yet as the story unfolds, we see their extraordinary impact on the rest of history.

As we take a deep dive into the Book of Ruth, we will see something else too. St. Augustine wrote, "The Old Testament is the New concealed; the New Testament is the Old revealed." This means the Old and New Testaments interpret each other—and we will see this connection in nearly every episode of the Book of Ruth. These connections are like underground rivers, transporting us directly to the story of Jesus and the early Church.

LIKE THE WORLD WIDE WEB

After all, the Bible is an integrated whole. I like to think of it as the first iteration of the World Wide Web! Words, phrases, concepts, ideas, references, patterns, and allusions are found in every chapter of every book in the Bible. They are like hyperlinks; we can "click" on a subject, statement, or word in one place and zoom to many other places in Scripture. Although written by multiple authors, in numerous languages and cultures, and compiled over centuries, the Bible is incredibly cross-referenced and coherent. Amazing!

I did not think this way in the early days of my walk with Christ. I read the Bible for content only. What does it say? What did God want me to do? What should I do? I saw the Bible as God's inspired Word written on two-dimensional paper. But now, the more I read and study the Bible, the more it takes on the look and feel of an expertly crafted quilt made up of patches, colors, and textures. In this way, the person, character, hope, promise, and impact of Jesus Christ is seen in every part of the quilt, as it were. He is in every story. I have come to see that the Bible is not just an anthology of 66 books. I see it now as a unified artistic narrative that will lead its reader directly to Jesus.

It is symbolic of our God's goodness that we would be given a beautiful and rich text that is such a cohesive whole. The Bible is not just a book of miracles; it is itself a miracle book. And *the book itself* is a message to us about the majesty of God. As the Word itself says, God is His Word (John 1:2).

We have a book we can read, mark, learn, and inwardly digest to our great benefit. And, like all deep dives into God's word, the deeper we go, the brighter and clearer it gets!

∾

God's creations are wonderfully made, and so is His written Word.

∾

THINKING MORE ABOUT IT

- How much of the Old and New Testament have you read?
- What do you think about the image of the Bible as a quilt instead of a flat piece of paper?
- What do you think about the quote from St. Augustine?

Deeper Dive: If your Bible has references in the margins, look up John 3:14–16. Follow the links wherever they lead.

3

A FAITH-LAST DECISION

In the days when the judges ruled, there was a
famine in the land, and a man of Bethlehem
in Judah went to sojourn in the country of
Moab, he and his wife and his two sons.
RUTH *1:1*

E limelech and his family stray 50 miles east of the
place they should have stayed. It is hard to fault
them; we can see the same "proneness to
wander" in our lives. We have all been 50 miles away from
God's will—at *least* that far! Elimelech's reasons for going
to the defiled and ungodly land of Moab are not based on
sinister motivations; he is trying to protect his family.
Perhaps he imagines he will find food in Moab and then
return when the famine in Bethlehem is over.

His decision is not faithless; it is faith-*last*. He puts the
faith and trust that he has in God, not in the first place,
but in the last place. It was a faith-last decision. I am very

familiar with *faith-last* decisions. Aren't you? We can all point to particular choices and turns in our lives that we make without thinking about God's perspective.

As Elimelech's forebears, Abraham and Sarah, discovered, leaving the Promised Land is almost always a mistake. Rarely do good things happen when we let faith give way to fear.

Science tells us there are two autonomic responses to threat and danger that govern humans: fight or flight. We either stand amid the danger, take whatever hard blows come, and fight our way through—or we leave. We turn and run. We flee.

In the Book of Ruth, Elimelech's family takes flight. It is hard to criticize them; we might do the same thing, caught in a life-threatening famine. But many in Bethlehem did *not* leave. They stand their ground because they are standing on God's earth, the land He had given them. The land God gives is holy. It is God's ground.

The Bible tells us that people of faith have more than the two standard autonomic responses to threat, danger, persecution, or calamity. We have more to choose from than fight or flight.

We can choose faith.

FAITH: THE FINAL FRONTIER

Remember what the Bible means by faith: "Now faith is the assurance of things hoped for, the conviction of things not seen" (Hebrews 11:1). This means that a person with biblical faith can look at circumstances and, instead of first asking, "What should I do?" we can wonder, "What is God doing?"

The lives of most people in the Bible are nowhere near perfect. Far from the stained-glass version we might see in Sunday school, their lives and families are sometimes a mess. A grown son usurps a king. A child raised by excellent parents and set apart from birth ends up a sexual predator. Almost everyone in the Bible makes a seriously bone-headed choice or two. I can relate. How about you?

The first few verses of Ruth show us how ordinary people of faith can get off track, make sudden wrong decisions, and abruptly find themselves far from where God wants them. But as the rest of Ruth's story shows, God can make things right. This is something for which God is known. He redeems bad decisions and restores joy that has slipped away. God does it over time. He does it through love.

This winding, circuitous journey toward redemption is a common theme of many sagas in the Bible. Given enough time, faith, courage, and tenacity, God's ordinary ways can turn faith-last choices to end in good.

But for now, let's take a lesson from Elimelech: When faith is not the first thing, it often becomes the last.

When faith is not the first thing we consider, it often becomes the last.

～

THINKING MORE ABOUT IT

- What is your greatest fear?
- When have you been "50 miles away from God?"
- Comment on the last line of this chapter.

Deeper Dive: Consider your most recent urges to fight or flight. How could Faith be the next best step?

4

THE MUD OF MOAB

So she set out from the place where she was with
her two daughters-in-law, and they went on
the way to return to the land of Judah.
RUTH 1:7

Elimelech and his family of four leave Bethlehem and travel to the land of the Moabites. Unfortunately, Elimelech dies soon after they arrive in Moab, and his wife, Naomi, is left with two sons who had been sickly from birth. Mahlon (which means *weak*), and the other is Chilion (which means, of all things, *annihilation*).

Their temporary furlough becomes a permanent assignment when the two young men marry Moabite wives. Mahlon marries Ruth, and Chilion marries Orpah. Marriage, according to Jewish law and custom, should not happen with pagan Moabites. They would never be allowed to resettle anywhere in Israel with these foreign, pagan women. After ten years, with no children from either marriage, both men die.

Of the six characters introduced in the opening verses, three are dead, and the remaining three face an unknown, precarious future. Naomi, Ruth, and Orpah—bereft of husbands, children, and security—are in trouble.

We may be tempted to condemn Elimelech for straying from his homeland in the face of a famine. Yet, if we're honest, most of us can remember a time when we've made a similar choice. Perhaps we made a quick decision based on the moment's urgency, only to learn later that it was wrong. Everyone has a story like this: well-intentioned decisions that go sideways. Sometimes snap decisions have permanent consequences; what we think is at our sole discretion can change our soul's direction.

In one of Jesus' most famous parables, we see a clear parallel. Once there was a father of two sons. The younger son demands his inheritance early and leaves for parts unknown. He throws himself into a bender of wine and women, but his luck quickly turns south. He runs out of money, food, and options. This rebel Jewish boy from a kosher family resorts to feeding pigs in the mud for a living, wishing he could eat what he had given them for dinner.

He is stuck in the mud with the pigs.

THERE IS NO PLACE LIKE HOME

Even at his lowest point, however, he never forgets his home. His luck has run out, and it doesn't turn around until he turns *himself* toward home. And when he does, he discovers that his father has already turned to welcome him home.

This is where Naomi finds herself. She can still remember Bethlehem. Perhaps she can remember the day Elimelech told her they were moving away from the land God had provided. Maybe she had even agreed to it. In any case, everything since then has gone wrong, and she is stuck in Moab mud.

So she turns around.

Naomi is out of luck but not out of options. She does the only thing she can to become unstuck. She firmly resolves that no matter the cost, she is going home.

She turns around.

There is a word in the Bible for this kind of turn: *Repent.* It means to turn around, go back, reverse, or change direction. Unlike the failed leaders in the Book of Judges before her, Naomi repents.

Naomi must go back. She knows that. Perhaps the long-suffering widow has always known that. Whether she had been the instigator of the escape plan to Moab, a willing participant, or a dutiful but reluctant wife, now she sets her mind on going home. She repents. A curse has burdened her, and it must be reversed. And for it to be redeemed, she must be restored to her town and land.

There is a saying that goes around churches sometimes: God loves you exactly where you are. This is a feel-good statement meant to give us the courage to repent and turn toward Him. But Naomi would say that it is only half right. She would add this: and He loves you enough not to leave you there.

Sometimes we just need to turn around and go home.

THINKING MORE ABOUT IT

- Where are you stuck? A career, relationships, choices?
- What is another term used for turning back?
- Paraphrase the last paragraph of the text above. How would that apply in your life?

Deeper Dive: Read the parable of the Prodigal Son in Luke 15:11–32.

5

LIFE, LOSS, AND THE BITTER TRUTH

But Naomi said to her two daughters-in-law,
"Go, return each of you to her mother's
house. May the LORD deal kindly with you,
as you have dealt with the dead and with me."
RUTH 1:8

The ancient story recorded in the Book of Ruth remains relevant because it is about real people facing real circumstances in a real and confusing world. Whether we are going places, we don't want to go, recovering from personal losses, fighting bitterness, moving forward in blind trust, or celebrating life's victories and vindications, every one of us can relate to some part of Ruth's story. We may carry the lingering effects of a wrong decision made earlier in life. We may bear wounds from a complicated or sad past. The Book of Ruth is as real as we are.

In the decade after Elimelech's death, his two sons found Moabite women to marry. One of them was named Ruth, and the other was Orpah. Tradition suggests the two women were sisters. We don't know what happened in ten years of marriage, but we know what did not happen: There were no children. In Bible times, childlessness was a private family grief; it cut off the possibility of perpetuating one's family name. And it foreclosed the hope that a parent might have that one of their descendants might be the coming Messiah.

No children, and then the two men die. Ruth and Orpah have lost their husbands, and Naomi, the text coldly reports, is "left without her two sons and her husband" (Ruth 1:5).

BECOMING BITTER

What are we to make of this tragedy? Perhaps through no fault of her own, Naomi is bankrupt. She has no family, save two daughters-in-law who are in the same socially tenuous position she is. Widows have no land to lease or sell to buy food and shelter. The three widows have no marriage prospects. None of them is a catch—and they know it.

Naomi is hopeless for the future because she's bitter about the past. She says to her daughters-in-law, "It is exceedingly bitter to me for your sake that the hand of the LORD has gone out against me" (v. 13). And later, once the widow has returned to Bethlehem and been welcomed home, Naomi decides to give up her name. "Do not call me Naomi," she corrects her friends, "call me Mara, for the Almighty has dealt very bitterly with me" (v. 20). Naomi means *pleasant* and Mara means *bitter.*

In my years as a pastor, I have been present with individuals and families through enormous tragedy and loss. I have been with parents grieving their stillborn children, a suddenly widowed husband, or a couple who had lost their only child to cancer. Early in my ministry, I buried John, a young husband in his mid-twenties, who had committed suicide. A week later, I conducted the burial service for his young wife, who, after his funeral, also killed herself. I drove to a lakeshore where the young couple used to fish. Their families stood on the shore and scattered the couple's ashes on the sand. As I stood next to the young man's father, I noticed he was using his boot to mix the dry sand from the lakeside beach with his son's and daughter-in-law's remains. *God,* I thought, *how can people get up and face their day after something like this?*

What keeps a survivor from becoming bitter, like Naomi? How do any of us make it without being embittered?

We know that we can expect to suffer in this life. Jesus himself says, "In this world, you will have trouble" (John 16:33). Faith or no faith, troubles still come. Jesus' disciples did not have a quiet, peaceful existence after they came to faith; their lives were complicated and even painful. But because God uses ordinary people, their lives —including their suffering—have extraordinary consequences. Yes, Jesus says we will have trouble in this world, but then He adds this next statement that changes everything: "but fear not, I have overcome the world."

If Naomi were able to tell us her story today, I wonder if she would conclude by saying, "Never change your name to Bitterness because in time, under God's gracious hand, you will want to change it back!"

For now, Naomi has much more to learn on this point (and by the end of the story, she'll have much more to teach us). What we know for now is that God is with her. She will not be left alone.

This is the ordinary way of God.

~

God will lead us <u>through</u> hard and bitter times.

~

THINKING MORE ABOUT IT

- With so much loss during COVID, how have you dealt with it?
- How is pain part of God's ordinary plan?
- Note and comment on these questions: What keeps a survivor from becoming bitter, like Naomi? How do any of us make it without being embittered?

Deeper Dive: Read Job 38–42. What did Job learn about suffering? (Job 42:1–5).

6

LOOK TO THE FACE, NOT TO
THE HAND

"I went away full, and the Lord has brought me
back empty. Why call me Naomi when the
Lord has testified against me, and the
Almighty has brought calamity upon me?"
Ruth 1:21

I f we believe the number-one goal in life is to live well, then suffering is an annoyance or even a sign of failure. Suffering is an intrusion, an interruption of the long series of successes we desire and deserve. If we believe our life's purpose and core value is to live well, anything bad that happens is of no value whatsoever.

Those who know the ordinary ways of God, however, understand hardship differently. When difficulties rattle believers to the bone, they also reveal a sovereign hand. Even though we feel out of control, we are cared for by a

God who is in control. His hand has come upon us. On the sunny side of hard times, this might sound trite and banal before our battle begins. But in the struggle, the trite becomes true: God loves us, and all this will work out for a greater good (see Rom. 8:28).

Consider Job. The Book of Job is so long that many readers never make it to the end. But the end is where Job learns two remarkable truths about suffering. First: God does not *cause* suffering but *allows* it. And second: Although God does not cause suffering, it reveals Him. Job says:

> *"I know that you can do all things,*
> *And that no purpose of yours can be thwarted.*
> *(Before) I had heard of you by the hearing of the ear,*
> *But now my eye sees you" (Job 42:5)*

Naomi will learn the same.

Naomi is an Israelite. She believes in the God of Abraham, Isaac, and Jacob. She blames God for her relatives' deaths. She believes the hand of God has come against her.

Maybe it is for this reason that she tries to dissuade her daughters-in-law from following her home. Ten years earlier, she had left Bethlehem with three men: her husband and two sons. The only thing she has to show now for this disastrous decade are three graves in Moab. Dante, poet composer of the *Divine Comedy*, captures the heart of Naomi's loss: "There is no greater sorrow than to recall in misery the time when we were happy." Naomi feels cursed by the hand of God.

THE HANDS AND THE FACE

When my wife and I were dating, I held her hand. I studied it. One day, I put a ring on her finger and married her. But it wasn't her hand that I fell in love with; it was her face. When I'm away from home and I think about her, I don't think about her hands, about what she has done; I picture her face—*who she is*. Everything I love about her is captured in her countenance.

When I turn toward my beloved wife, I look at her face, not her hands.

Of course, we know God has no physical body. He does not have physical hands, even though we read in the Psalms that all creation is His handiwork (see 19:1). He does not have a face, even though Psalm 27:8 tells us to seek it. These word pictures—hands and face—are not *real*, but they are *true*. They are metaphors to help us fathom God's power and His connection to us.

This is what Naomi will learn. Right now, at the beginning of the story, she is looking at the *hand* of God and what she fears He has done. She believes that the hand of God has brought pain and suffering to her. After 10 long years and 50 long miles from home, she has forgotten how to seek His face. She comes from a people of faith accustomed to hard times, but she has forgotten their faith lessons. Her ancestors, who endured hardship *and* loved God, would tell her to look not for His hand but His face.

God deserves our worship not for what He does but for who He is.

THINKING MORE ABOUT IT

- Read the quote from Dante and comment whether it is true or not.
- Look to the face, not the hand. How might this perspective change your circumstances?
- In what area of life have you focused on the "hand of God?"

7

LEAVING AND CLEAVING

Then they lifted up their voices and wept again.
And Orpah kissed her mother-in-law, but
Ruth clung to her.
RUTH 1:14

Although they may not know it, God is continually weaving and working for people He loves. Everyone in the Book of Ruth is a beneficiary of God's love and mercy, even if they do not realize it. He is a constant force of love and protection who hovers over the lives of every named character. And though some do not even know Him, as may be the case with Ruth, that does not stop God from intervening on their behalf.

We should remember this, a regular theme in the Bible: God moves on and for His people with or without their recognition of Him. The Scriptures tell us many times that even when we forget about God, He never forgets us. He never forsakes us, even when we reject Him. Knowing this truth deep within gives us tremendous security.

As the three women leave Orpah and Ruth's Moabite hometown, Naomi tries three times to dissuade her daughters-in-law from going to Israel with her. She can promise them nothing. They should return to their Moabite mothers and try to find new husbands. And in the end, Orpah does turn for home—but Ruth stays. The story says that Ruth "clung" to Naomi. This is the same Hebrew word translated in Genesis 2:24 to describe what a new husband is to do with his new wife: He is to *cleave* to her. We don't use it much today but cleave means "to attach firmly." It also has a near opposite meaning—to split—but in the case of husbands and wives and Ruth and Naomi, it means "to hold fast."

Orpah leaves. Ruth cleaves.

Ruth's act of loyalty and dedication is one of the most surprising and consequential moments in the entire Bible. She cannot know the impact this act of love will have on her future. By it, Naomi will be protected and cared for in her old age. Through it, Ruth will meet Boaz and bear a son in King David's—and eventually Jesus'—family tree. From it, a ray of hope shines out of the dark time of the Judges.

In a single unexpected act of dedication and commitment to another's well-being, the course of the future is changed.

This is how God uses the ordinary commitments we make to other people, to our families, and, of course, to our spouses.

God is in the process of repairing Naomi's past mistakes and bringing her family line back to Israel. He will also graft the Moabite race into His family, thereby setting off a chain of events that will lead to the birth of Israel's greatest king—and then finally lead to the King of kings a thousand years later. God is also establishing Bethlehem as a place where hope is born.

All of this hinges on Ruth's commitment to Naomi.

But what about Orpah? What happens to her? She returns to her people and her pagan life and is never heard from again in the pages of Scripture. She does appear in Midrash commentaries on this story, and the Rabbis are not kind to her. (The Midrash is Jewish commentary, interpretations, and thoughts about the Hebrew Bible texts collected between 200 and 1200 AD.) They surmise that, when she returned to Moab, Orpah suffered hundreds of indignities. One source claims she had a son who became Goliath's father!

This is speculation, of course, but it does highlight for us the power of human choice.

The Book of Ruth has strong forward momentum toward redemption. God moves and shapes the future according to His will, and He uses ordinary people. This is His way. But the sovereignty of God's actions does not absolve us of personal responsibility for our choices. Orpah was entirely responsible for her actions, which took her out of the redemption drama God was writing.

~

God uses our commitments to redeem our present and the future.

~

THINKING MORE ABOUT IT

- In your struggles and circumstances, are you leaving (Orpah) or cleaving (Ruth)?
- Their personal choices had a significant impact on both women. How can you see similar implications in your own life?
- When was the last "fork in the road" major decision that you had to make? How did you know what to do?

8

LOYALTY MAKES PROMISES

*"For where you go I will go, and where you lodge
I will lodge. Your people shall be my people,
and your God my God. Where you die I will
die, and there I will be buried. May the LORD
do so to me and more also if anything but
death parts me from you."*
RUTH 1:16–17

R uth's short song is beautiful to read and wonderful to share with a spouse or very good friend. It has sometimes been used as wedding vows, and for a good reason. Did you notice that each of the song's lines is a promise? And line by line, *each promise is a deeper level of commitment than the line before*. Ruth will go with Naomi, then she will stay with Naomi, then she will join Naomi's community, then Ruth will believe in

Naomi's God, and finally, she will be buried beside Naomi's grave.

1. She will go with Naomi to Bethlehem. This was an exercise of courage and trust. Neither Naomi nor Ruth can know the good things that will unfold upon Naomi's return. Regardless, Ruth goes where Naomi goes.

2. She will stay where Naomi stays. Ruth and Naomi will become housemates in Bethlehem. As a pair of childless widows from two different generations, their mornings will likely be filled with sharing urgent ideas for survival. And their evenings will brim with praises to God for the day-by-day supply of food they can find or forage.

3. Ruth will join Naomi's tribe. Ruth is a pagan and a Moabite. Her people have a dark history with Naomi's people, the Israelites. And, as she accompanies her mother-in-law, she knows with every step toward Bethlehem, that she is taking a step away from her old world. Through her immigration to Bethlehem, Ruth binds herself to Naomi's people, as her song proclaims. When she marries Boaz, she is fully assimilated to the Israelites.

4. Ruth will bind herself to the God of Israel. Ruth becomes a worshiper of the God of Abraham, Isaac, and Jacob. This is the most remarkable of all Ruth's promises. After all, what does she know about Naomi's God? We don't precisely know, but it's almost certain she doesn't like everything she can see for herself: Naomi's life turned sour and bitter. Her faithful Jewish husband, Mahlon, was sickly and unable to conceive with her. She is a too-young

widow. And yet, even with all these marks seemingly against Him, Ruth is willing to "sign on" with Naomi's God. He will be Ruth's God, too.

5. Ruth will live the rest of her life by Naomi's side—even after her mother-in-law dies. She is willing to die where Naomi dies and be buried beside her. She won't wait for Naomi to die of old age and then return to Moab. No, the Moabitess will join herself to a new race and a new religion. And eventually, when Naomi dies, Ruth will live out her life until she perishes too. Then, as she promises, she will be buried alongside her mother-in-law's remains, resting beside her for all time.

PROMISES ARE A ROADMAP

The 1662 Edition of *The Book of Common Prayer* contains the most elegant and beautiful vows ever composed for any occasion. They are familiar to all of us.

> I M. take thee N. to my wedded wife, to have and to hold, from this day forward, for better for worse, for richer for poorer, in sickness and in health, to love and to cherish, till death us do part, according to God's holy ordinance; and thereto I plight thee my troth.

(The archaic language of the last phrase means, simply, to pledge my fidelity; it is akin to the word 'betroth'. It is beautiful.)

I have presided over many wedding ceremonies, especially of young, starry-eyed couples standing before the altar in church. There, in front of God and the people who love and support them, they make truly courageous vows and promises to each other. I am involved in this ritual only to give the lines of each vow to them so that they can speak them to each other. I often imagine that the line by line promises and vows they recite to each other are actually a description of the challenges and fortunes that await them.

And when I look out into the congregation and see older, married couples holding each other's hand during this part of the service, I know that they know what the couple does not know yet. Namely, that the good and the bad, the rich and the poor, the sickness and the health will all happen to them. And they will make it through these fortunes and fouls together because they have made the vow to do it together.

Ruth speak her song like a set of vows. And the song is the roadmap of events to follow. Ruth's poem is, in effect, the plan for her life, from the time she vows it to Naomi to the day she gives birth to her firstborn son, Obed. This is the power of promises—they shape our future as we fulfill them.

Ruth makes her promise to Naomi. She is declaring that no matter what, she will remain with her. Ruth's marvelous song is, in a word, exquisite.

~

Through God, the promises we make chart the course we take.

∿

THINKING MORE ABOUT IT

- Why do you think Ruth was willing to go?
- Do you have a plan for your life? Where does it lead?
- How do our promises chart the course of our life?

9

THE STRENGTH OF A MAN

. . . a worthy man of the clan of Elimelech, whose
name was Boaz.
RUTH 2:1

The first chapter of Ruth begins with a looming famine and ends with an abundant harvest. God has acted to save His people. Now, during the harvest, we are introduced to a relative of Naomi's named Boaz. The story described Boaz as a worthy man. In some translations, he is a man of "standing" or "great wealth." And he has a backstory all his own.

Do you remember Rahab, a prostitute in Jericho, who hid Joshua's spies when they came to reconnoiter the Promised Land? (See Joshua 2–6.) She played a significant role in Israel's victory over Jericho. She and her household were protected from harm when the Israelite army marched around the city and toppled the walls. They were saved and lived among God's people from that day forward.

Later, Rahab had a son named Boaz. (Rahab and Ruth are two of only five women—just three are mentioned by name—to appear in Jesus' genealogy recorded in Matthew's Gospel.) She must have done something right when it came to raising him because Boaz is *worthy*.

As we'll see, he shows exceptional restraint. He does not command anyone, including women (and most especially Ruth). He seems to understand that, though he is of the stronger sex—his name means *strength*—he need not be forceful or demanding.

Boaz never assumes he has the upper hand with Ruth. Quite the opposite: He is humbled that she pays him any notice. When he wakes to find the young woman lying at the foot of his bed, he does not take advantage of her. Many men would read Ruth's proximity as an invitation for promiscuity; some even work overtime to exploit vulnerable women. But this worthy man is different.

From the moment he enters Ruth's story, Boaz is merely trying to make life better for her, seeking a way for the Lord to bless her for the kindness she has shown to his widowed relative. He has no reason to expect he will be the one to provide that blessing.

This worthy man lives a life of generosity, humility, strength, and usefulness to God. God uses this ordinary man to achieve extraordinary things.

BLESSED ARE THE MEEK

There is a biblical word for this kind of person—one not often used but, when it is, usually misunderstood. The term is *meek*. Boaz is a meek man. He exudes gentle strength from a place of deep humility and a desire to be of service.

What does it mean to be meek? The best way to understand this rarely used word is to imagine training a wild horse. Trainers refer to the training sessions as "meeking" a horse. Trainers meek a wild stallion by channeling his power toward loyal service rather than unruly independence. This is the only way he can be useful to his master. Meeking a horse tames the steed's innate instinct to run recklessly and brings him under the master's control. The horse retains his breed's spirit, courage, and power, but now he is disciplined and responsive to the slightest nudge or pressure from his rider's leg.

Jesus uses this word to describe one of the first attributes of a devoted disciple: "Blessed are the meek, for they shall inherit the earth" (Matthew 5:5). The apostle Paul ascribes this quality to the Lord, speaking of "the meekness and gentleness of Christ" (2 Corinthians 10:1).

Boaz is meek. He doesn't have anything to prove. He is strong, yes, but his power is under the control of kindness, humility, and service.

It may be that Boaz's strength became legendary among his descendants. Solomon, his great-great-great-grandson, may have had his strong-but-meek forbearer in mind when he named one of the two bronze pillars in the Temple "Boaz" (see 1 Kings 7:21). Think about that! Meekness is power, strength, and stability under God's control.

~

God calls men to serve with strength, kindness, and humility.

~

THINKING MORE ABOUT IT

- How do you think Rahab's past taught Boaz about being meek?
- In our society today, is meekness a desired quality? Why?
- How does Jesus show a perfect example of strength IN meekness?

Deeper Dive: Read Joshua 2–6 and the conquest of Jericho. Meet Rahab.

10

ARE THERE COINCIDENCES?

> *... and she happened to come to the part of the field belonging to Boaz, who was of the clan of Elimelech.*
>
> RUTH 2:3

Jesus began the Parable of the Good Samaritan with these words: "Now by chance a priest was going down that road . . ." Jesus used the Greek word *"sunkurion"* which, if it were fully translated, would mean, "occurring together with the supreme authority." In other words, a coincidence is something that occurs by God's intentional arrangement of circumstances.

Indeed, the Bible writers do not see anything that happens as mere chance apart from God's providential will. Yet, at the same time, they write about human-instigated actions: People act and react, each according to their own free will. Every person has *agency*. No one is a robot. God gives free will to each living person—and at the same time, every person's actions are under Almighty God's providential rule.

This is the ordinary way of God.

How can these two seemingly irreconcilable views both be right? For indeed they are. Both God's will and humanity's free will are at work in the course of human affairs. The second chapter of Ruth is an example of this dynamic.

Consider this first: God is mentioned in this story, but He never speaks. There are no miracles, signs, or wonders. I've argued this story is meaningful because its characters *are* so ordinary. The God behind all things acts in everyday ways.

Secondly, all the story's main characters are on stage by the end of chapter two—all together for the first time—and as the chapter unfolds, they each make plans, determine their courses of action, and react to certain events of their own accord.

It *just so happens* that, when Naomi and Ruth return to Bethlehem, the "City of Bread" is living up to its name. It's harvest time, and there is plenty of food. So Ruth decides to go to the fields to glean among the reapers. It *just so happens* that Ruth works her way onto Boaz's fields. Boaz *just so happens* to be in the area and sees her. He asks about the young woman, and it *just so happens* that the young man he asks knows more than enough about Ruth to capture the wealthy older landowner's attention.

Then Boaz breaks tradition and approaches Ruth directly. He encourages her to be prudent about where she does her work; for her protection, she should stay with the women of the field. Boaz then instructs the young male reapers to be a little less efficient in their harvesting and leave a little more for the new girl. When Ruth returns home with an *ephah* (about 25 pounds) of barley, Naomi is overwhelmed and asks where she could have found such bounty. Ruth tells her mother-in-law that the man in whose field she worked is named Boaz. And it *just so happens* that Boaz is Naomi's relative.

That's a string of "just-so-happens" that would never have happened without human effort and could never have happened without God's unseen, providential hand working in His ordinary ways.

LUCKY YOU

If we each look closely at our personal history, we discover the same dynamic at work. With the gift of hindsight, we can see a tautly scripted drama being played out with a much larger purpose in mind. Often amid the drama, we do not know the purpose behind God's plan. But with the gift of hindsight, we can see there are no coincidences or lucky breaks; there is only the hand and heart of God bringing you and me and our lives to a redemptive end, making our lives count for something.

In the Book of Ruth, Naomi is empty, but she will be made full. Ruth is a racial and religious outsider, but she will be fully grafted into the family and God's people through marriage. Boaz is a single man with, as we discover, lots of competition from younger men. His mother was a prostitute who later became a wartime convert to the God of Israel.

Are these coincidences? Are they only "just-so-happens"? No.

If we were to jump ahead right now to view this chapter with the gift of hindsight, we would see our extraordinary God accomplishing extraordinary things through ordinary people. Ruth gives birth to Obed. He will become Jesse's father, who becomes David's father—and David is in the lineage that leads to Jesus! It is a sequence of events that could not have happened without God's providential hand at work.

There are no "just-so-happens" in the walk of faith. There is only the providence of God.

∼

All things work together for good for those who love the Lord.

∼

THINKING MORE ABOUT IT

- Think of a time you thought you were lucky. Can you now see it was God at work?
- How is hindsight helpful in seeing God's providential hand?
- As you read Ruth's story, do you think she was just lucky? Right time, right place?

11

RACISM AND THE BIBLE

"She is the young Moabite woman who came
back with Naomi from the country of Moab."
RUTH 2:6

Racism is an ugly word. It connotes the idea of a race of people feeling superior to another. Being called a "racist" is a cutting insult. Using racial slurs is regarded as hate speech. Given the attention to the matter and the ferocity of the debate, we might think that it is a new problem that society is trying to quickly correct.

But racial divisions go back to the dawn of history. It is woven into the ancient world's culture, and, as such, it is reflected in the stories and descriptions of people, nations, and communities. But the Book of Ruth is very different from any other story of its day. The story challenges the entire idea of racial identity and divisions. It would have been a surprising jolt to the systemic racism inherent in the ancient world. This is one of the many reasons why this short book is so powerful.

In the time of the Judges, when Ruth was written, nationalities and racial identities were nearly synonymous. If you lived in Moab, you were of the Moabite race. If you lived in Israel, you were a Jew. We should keep this in mind as we look at race in the Book of Ruth.

The Book of Ruth mentions Ruth's nationality far more often than it needs to: five times in four chapters. We know from the first verses in the story that she is from Moab, yet the writer keeps telling us over and over again, repeatedly reminding us that she is outside a covenant relationship with God. She is a foreigner.

Ancient Moab was the quintessential no-go zone for Israelites. Although they lived barely 50 miles away, Moabites were feared enemies, a despised people. As we find in the following verse, the Moabites were pure pagans, and, given their sordid beginnings, God's people were to have no connection with them. Deuteronomy 23:3 is specific:

> No Ammonite or Moabite may enter the
> assembly of the LORD. Even to the tenth
> generation, none of them may enter the
> assembly of the LORD forever.

The Law also states the Israelites should not welcome anyone from Moab. (Leviticus 21:17–21)

When we recall the sweet and loyal sentiments of Ruth's song—that Naomi's God will be her God, too—we must also realize how difficult it will be to effect this change. It will be impossible without the proactive work of Boaz, the kinsman-redeemer. In order for Ruth to participate in the Abrahamic Covenant, her faith status will have to change. She will have to be reclassified, grafted into the new line of faith. She will need, in other words, to be born again.

WE ARE ALL OUTSIDERS

It is remarkable that so brief a book could be such an unmistakable herald of the Gospel of Jesus Christ to come 1,500 years later. The Book of Ruth and the Cross of Christ are both good news for outsiders. In Paul's letter to the Ephesians, we learn that each of us starts in virtually the same position as Ruth:

> Remember that you were ... alienated from
> the commonwealth of Israel and
> strangers to the covenants of promise,
> having no hope and without God in the
> world. But now in Christ Jesus you who
> once were far off have been brought near
> by the blood of Christ. ... And he came
> and preached peace to you who were far
> off and peace to those who were near. ...

> So then you are no longer strangers and
> aliens, but you are fellow citizens with
> the saints and members of the household
> of God (Ephesians 2:12–13,17,19).

I n a biblical sense, we are *all* from Moab. We are all outsiders. As Paul famously declares in Romans 3:23, "All have sinned and fall short of the glory of God." We are all "strangers" and "aliens." But through Christ, we are in the family of God.

We would do well to remember this in our current day and time. There is no one race, ethnicity, color, or culture that is closer to God than any other.

A vision near the end of the New Testament describes the heavenly throne where people worship and praise the Lord Jesus (see Revelation 7). They come from every family, tribe, ethnicity, and nation. Together they are one people, a kingdom of priests. Believing Moabites are certainly in the room. No people, group, skin color, tribal heritage, or ethnicity is excluded.

By the end of the biblical story racism is erased.

∽

God's way will erase the racial divisions in our life.

∽

THINKING MORE ABOUT IT

- Christ died for ALL. How would that be good news for the world to hear?
- What areas do you need to work on accepting others?
- How does this chapter challenge or change your thoughts on racism?

12

OUR SILENT PARTNER

Then she said, "I have found favor in your eyes,
my lord, for you have comforted me and
spoken kindly to your servant, though I am
not one of your servants."
RUTH 2:13

wo books in the Old Testament are named for the women in the lead roles: the Book of Ruth and the Book of Esther. While they are two vastly different stories, each is a mirror image of the other. Esther is an ascendant queen; Ruth, a lowly peasant. Esther is a Jewess who marries a Gentile; Ruth is a Gentile who marries an Israelite. The Book of Esther opens with a feast; the Book of Ruth with a famine. And Esther's story ends with an enemy's death, while Ruth's culminates in a baby's birth.

But they share something in common: In both, God is a background player. This is certainly not to say that He is unimportant. On the contrary, He is everywhere, woven into every person's attitudes and actions and every scene's details. Yet God is mentioned not once in the Book of Esther, and in the Book of Ruth, He never speaks, and no one prays. In both stories, God acts behind the scenes in the lives of famous people (Esther) and unknown, ordinary people (Ruth) to protect, preserve, and provide for His people.

When the long-time Israelite family left Israel for Moab, they were leaving God's land. We can be sure that, as when Elimelech, then Mahlon, and then Chilion died, Naomi must have wondered whether God had left her when she left Bethlehem.

How often have we felt that way? We follow the course of our life and make the decisions that we think are best. Then troubles come on us. We feel as though darkness surrounds us. We have all been there, and we have all felt, in those times, the way we never want to feel. Alone.

WE ARE NEVER ALONE

The Book of Ruth reveals to us a deep and mysterious truth: God will not leave us. He may move to the background. He may be concealed for reasons we can never know. But, as each character in Ruth could attest, God does not leave us. He may not speak, but He is never far away.

Psalm 139 assures us of this:

> Where shall I go from your Spirit?
> Or where shall I flee from your presence?
> If I ascend to heaven, you are there!
> If I make my bed in Sheol, you are there!
>   (Vs. 7–8)

These are such powerful lines of poetry. As a pastor, I have read parts of this psalm during many counseling sessions with members of my church. It brings comfort to those who feel lost or alone. It tells us that there is never an "alone time" for a believer. God will always be with us. He will stay with us.

Ruth's great-grandson David wrote these lines from Psalm 139. I wonder if he had the family story of Naomi and Ruth in mind.

The story of Ruth is a story about the sovereignty of God. Looking back on the events of Ruth's experience, we can apply these truths to our own lives in our own time.

God may be silent, but He is not absent. God may never speak, but He is always active.

This is the masterstroke of Ruth's story. Our God's power and presence are beyond our understanding, and sometimes, we never know the purpose or plan until the end. The lesson Ruth can teach us is an important one.

God, even though silent, is never absent.

~

THINKING MORE ABOUT IT

- What statement in this chapter is the most comforting?
- Read the passage from Psalm 139. What is your take-away?
- What do you think about this phrase? *"God may be silent, but He is not absent."*

Deeper Dive: Read Psalm 139 and the Book of Esther.

13

ORDINARY PEOPLE

And at mealtime, Boaz said to her, "Come here
and eat some bread and dip your morsel in
the wine." So she sat beside the reapers, and
he passed to her roasted grain.
RUTH 2:14

I t is supper time in Bethlehem. After a day filled
with gleanings and blessings, Boaz and Ruth sit
with the other reapers to share a meal. Bread. Wine.
Roasted grain. Ruth is keeping a polite and appropriate
distance from Boaz. He is sending an unmistakable signal
of interest in her. Take note of this: One of the most deci-
sive meetings in the Bible happens at a picnic. Nothing
fancy. It is not a state dinner with royalty or dignitaries. It
is just a common group of sweaty people taking a break
for some bread and wine. Pretty ordinary.

The ways of God are often this ordinary. We may look for
flashing signs and wonders, but few of us ever see them.

God is more circumspect in most of our circumstances. We may sing a song that claims, "He's got the whole world in His hands" and never actually see His hands at work. Because guess what? He is not on the hook to show off or prove His omnipotent powers every day in every way. And that's okay. As we look through the Bible's history of faithful people living out the days of their lives, we discover a wonderfully refreshing and reassuring truth: God is present and at work in the mundane details. This is extraordinary.

THE TRUTH IN A TWEET

The simple act of Christian corporate worship is one of the most important, ordinary things we do to effect change in our culture, our community, and in our own life. How does my experience of worship change me or change the world? Simple. It removed us from the center of our lives. It reminds us that God was here always and will be here always long before we appeared on the planet. And He will still be God and King long after we are dust.

Paul David Tripp recently put this truth in a tweet:

Corporate worship is designed to cause you to run from the kingdom of self and run to the kingdom of God, to dethrone yourself and to give your life to celebrating and serving the King of Kings everywhere you are and in whatever you do.

One of the Book of Ruth's underlying messages is that God's ways can be pretty down-to-earth. The people in the story are not winners or champions; they are ordinary folk. The events are not full of action or danger or adventure; they are mostly just day-to-day life. But in Ruth and our lives today, God can use anything and anyone to accomplish any aspect of His will.

In the classic daily devotional *My Utmost for His Highest,* Oswald Chambers writes, "All of God's people are ordinary people who have been made extraordinary by the purpose He has given them."[1]*

If we have not attained the stellar career we hoped or strived for; if we have not made the kind of money or earned the accolades we dreamed of; if we are, in a word, *ordinary*, that does not mean we are insignificant. Just the opposite. Our ordinary lives *mean something* because God's ordinary way is to use people just like us in our everyday circumstances. He does this all the time in the Bible. He does this in the Book of Ruth. And He still does today.

We are not extras in God's movie, thrown in for background color. We are not ornaments; we are instruments in His hand. Regardless of the setting, scene, or circumstance, He can use us. He *will* use us.

Oswald Chambers goes on to say, "Never protest by saying, 'If only I were somewhere else!'" This is the plea of a person without faith. Ruth's story demonstrates that ordinary lives count, that all lives count. Every life has meaning and can be part of God's plan and purpose.

~

God uses ordinary people to accomplish His extraordinary purpose.

~

THINKING MORE ABOUT IT

- How does the statement that all God's people are ordinary but used for His extraordinary purpose relate to you?
- Read the last quote from Oswald Chambers. Have you ever thought this way?
- How has God used you in an ordinary way recently?

14

THE BIGGEST WORD IN THE WORLD

When she rose to glean, Boaz instructed his
young men, saying, "Let her glean even
among the sheaves, and do not reproach her."
RUTH 2:15

There is a Hebrew word in the Book of Ruth that has no direct English equivalent, and it is the key to understanding every exchange between the principal characters: *hesed*. Many people know that there is more than one word for "love," but hesed is not one of them. Its meaning is more substantial than "love"; there is weight and permanence to it. Hesed has heft. We can come closer to its essence with a compound: unfailing love. Loving-kindness, eternal, limitless, faithful love comes relatively close to the idea of hesed.

I once heard another preacher suggest that hesed contains all the fruits of the Spirit: love, joy, peace, patience, kindness, goodness, faithfulness, gentleness, and self-control. That's a lot of meaning packed into such a small word!

Hesed describes a deep and abiding friendship in which a person in a position of power commits to lovingly and mercifully supplying someone's critical needs. David and Jonathan's friendship, forged while young David serves Prince Jonathan's father, King Saul, is hesed.

God's covenant love has often been described this way in the Scriptures. It does not depend on our response. It's love that is unconditional, generous, grace-filled, and full of mercy. It is one-way love. Hesed runs deeper than erotic love, further than friendship love, and stronger than marital love. Acting out of hesed for His people is the ordinary way of God. It is impossible to have hesed and *not* act on it.

The Apostle John codified this thought in a very provocative phrase which should be held close in every believers heart.

> If anyone has material possessions and sees a brother or sister in need but has no pity on them, how can the love of God be in that person? (I John 3:17)

Hesed is beyond the love of societal or legal expectations, relational or familial responsibilities, and ever-shifting passions and impulses.

ONE WAY LOVE

The great beauty of the Book of Ruth is that we see hesed in action.

It is sometimes said that the Book of Ruth is a love story. It is not. The word "love" is never used. More thoroughly and accurately, it is a hesed story of incredible, faithful, steadfast, unwavering, committed, generous, grace-filled, unconditional favor toward another person. The word "love," even though it is a many-splendored thing, doesn't do it justice.

- When Ruth initiates her harvest gleaning to provide food for her mother-in-law, that is hesed.
- When Boaz asks the young men to provide for the Moabitess, that is hesed. When Ruth presents herself to Boaz that night on the threshing floor, that was a form of hesed.[1]*
- Hesed is the favor between Ruth and Naomi.
- And we will see hesed between Boaz and the young bride. She was committed to him. He fulfills the role of her committed husband. He loves her, provides for her, and protects her.

It's tempting to believe that Ruth was motivated to stay with Naomi for her (Ruth's) own sake—maybe she disliked her options back in Moab—or for Mahlon's sake, as a family obligation to her dead husband's mother. But this was not the case. We find her care and loyalty hard to believe because it's hard to imagine a real person with this kind of steadfast love for anyone other than herself.

Ruth had *hesed* and acted on it. Hesed must find a way to be demonstrated, otherwise it is just a sentimental idea.

We have no equivalent word for *hesed* in the English language and we are the poorer for it. But we do have a comprehensive example of *hesed* in action; we have the living loving-kindness of the ministry of Jesus. His Gospel message and His Gospel ministry is the best and highest example of the one-way love of God. The well-known Gospel declaration of John 3:16 is rooted in *hesed*. The eternal, limitless, faithful love sent Jesus to the cross to offer his life for all humanity.

Jesus had hesed—He was hesed—and He acted on it.

∾

God's ordinary way calls us to extraordinary loving ways.

∾

THINKING MORE ABOUT IT

- 1. Have you experienced a hesed relationship?
- 2. Would you agree that the Book of Ruth is not a love story?
- 3. Can you see the perfect hesed in Jesus?

OUR REDEEMER RELATIVE

*And Naomi said to her daughter-in-law, "May
he be blessed by the LORD, whose kindness
has not forsaken the living or the dead!"
Naomi also said to her, "The man is a close
relative of ours, one of our redeemers."*
RUTH 2:20

This story's contribution to the Bible's revelation of God's salvation cannot be overstated. It shows us exactly what it means to need and to secure the services of a redeemer. Ephesians 2 reminds us that we are foreigners excluded from the inheritance of God's people.[1]* We do not belong. We have no rights, no lot, no inheritance.

But after the redeemer does his work, the foreigner is in the family. The barbarian becomes a bride.

How does this happen? The answer to this question is the invaluable contribution of the Book of Ruth. Fifteen hundred or so years before the time of Christ, the Bible established the concept of the "kinsman-redeemer." We see it mentioned in Deuteronomy 24, but we don't see the practical work of redeeming something or someone until the climax of Ruth's story. This is a stunning fact.

The Book of Ruth is the Bible's *only* example of the kinsman-redeemer law affecting human lives. Without this story, neither Jews nor Christians would have a real-life example of the law in practice (except, as Christians claim, for the redeeming work of Jesus Christ).

This is such a startling point that I want to make it in a different way.

The Bible has a long, continuous narrative arc from the early chapters of Genesis to Revelation. In this storyline, the single biggest question hovering over the face of creation is how Adam and Eve's sons and daughters will find their way back to the Garden, back to God. How will they return to paradise and a free and full eternal life with God? They have sinned. They have separated themselves from their Creator. They are held in bondage by their actions and Satan's activity. He has stolen their identity. They are children of the Father and heirs of the Kingdom, but an evil captor prevents them from finding their way home. How will they be saved and returned to God?

This is the underlying, overarching question of the Bible.

A REDEEMER AKIN TO US

God introduced an idea first to the Jews: a person, a kinsman-redeemer, who could free people from slavery, bondage, debt, and the need for vengeance. This person must be "akin" to them to be a member of the family. But he must also have superior means and ability to pay the price and perform the rescue.

Even though Deuteronomy introduces the idea of a "kinsman-redeemer," the Old Testament has only a single record of this provision applied in human history: in the Book of Ruth. There is but one example in the Bible of how it works in real life. This is the crucial role played by the Book of Ruth in the biblical narrative. We understand from Deuteronomy the need for a ransom to free the land, save a bride, and sustain the family name, but we see it happen in Ruth.

So how does it work?

The redeemer must redeem the land by agreeing to take on the debt burden, making a public promise that he will pay the required price. Once the price is set and paid, the redeemer can take full possession of the land. And once that is done (see Ruth 4), Ruth can become Boaz's bride, and they can consummate their marriage that very night.

This is extraordinary. Boaz changes the course of Ruth's life and brings her into the fellowship of the Covenant. She will no longer be called a Moabite. From that point forward, she will be an Israelite—and their children will be heirs of the Covenant.

These extraordinary things are accomplished in ordinary ways. This is the ordinary way of God.

It is almost too beautiful for words, but Boaz's redemption of Ruth is a foreshadowing of what Christ does for all God's people who are, by faith, "grafted" into the Covenant. Jesus speaks about his intention to give his life as a ransom for many. (Mark 10:45). He enters our public arena to make his pledge. He offers himself on the Cross as full payment for our sins in a public display of sacrifice. After that, the Church he has paid so dear a price to redeem will be called the "bride of Christ."

~

God's way can free us from the sorrows and burdens of past sins.

~

THINKING MORE ABOUT IT

- We call Jesus our Redeemer. In what way is He also our Kinsman?
- What is a "foreshadowing?" How does Boaz foreshadow Jesus?
- Why is the church referred to as the "bride of Christ" and not the "wife of Christ?"

Deeper Dive: Read Deuteronomy 24 and Ephesians 2.

16

OUR FREE WILL

So she went down to the threshing floor and did
just as her mother-in-law had commanded
her.
RUTH 3:6

As we have seen, there are no coincidences in the walk of faith. But this fact does not negate the efforts we must make.

God does His part to work His extraordinary purposes. But so does Naomi. And so does Ruth. Even though everything depends on God, Naomi and Ruth work as if everything depends on them. Naomi dispatches Ruth to the threshing floor with specific instructions. And Ruth, risking her reputation, chooses to follow through. Naomi has her will, which she imposes on Ruth, and Ruth has her own choice, which she superimposes on that!

But what about God's will?

People often wonder how human free will works alongside God's providential will. Endless debates ensue. How can a person's actions be "free" and, concurrently, determined by God? It is a mystery impossible to grasp fully, yet it is the way the God of the Bible writes history: as a cooperative partnership between His action and human agency.

One way to get our minds around this tension is to imagine both the modern author of a story and her story's characters. The author knows what the book is about, and he knows the direction of the plot-line. She knows what names will emerge as heroes and who will fall from grace. She knows the plot and subplots, the beginning and end, but until she is actively writing the story as it unfolds, the intricate ins and out and twists and turns are an open question. A good author knows the story's arc but leaves a lot of wiggle room for the characters to make surprising choices.

HIS WILL AND OUR WAY

Now consider the story from inside. The characters are alive *within the storyline*. They are bound by decisions the author has already made about time and space. The characters are "born" in a place at a point in time, *inside* a story that's already happening. Within those constraints, they make choices. They have agency. They speak for themselves, make their mistakes, and live their lives by taking actions they initiate and by responding to actions undertaken by others.

Our free will and God's divine providence exist in a similar dynamic. Both act. Both exert forces to move the story forward.

Our created order is God's handiwork. We are His handiwork inside that creation. He is Author of all life! He makes space for us to make choices to propel our storyline forward, but He knows the end of the grand, ultimate story. It is, after all, His to begin with.

We are people of free will. Each person, by their very existence, has God-given freedom. We cry out for those freedoms when they are taken away. And the Author of our lives joins us in this cry. Every person is created to choose the steps they take today and tomorrow.

All those steps lead somewhere, as we see in the Book of Ruth. Orpah is free to go her way and she does. And while Jewish Midrash is not kind to her, we can honestly say that she chose her path and walked it. Ruth is free to make her choices. Naomi and Boaz, too. So are we. But the Book of Ruth also shows us that before, behind, and beside every character is God's providential power.

Yes, we are free. Yes, God is sovereign. It is a mystery.

$\sim$

God uses our everyday efforts to accomplish His will.

～

THINKING MORE ABOUT IT

- How is the example of the Author (God) and character (you) helpful in understanding of free will?
- Do you feel a tension between your will and God's?
- How does having choices lead you to a deeper trust in God?

17

WINGS

*"Spread your wings over your servant, for you
are a redeemer."*
RUTH 3:9

R uth chapters 2 and 3 should be read in tandem
because they mirror and magnify each other.

In chapter 2, in the harvest fields, Boaz pays
unusual attention to Ruth. In chapter 3, on the threshing
floor, Ruth pays unusual attention to Boaz (she proposes
marriage!).

In chapter 2, Ruth is humbled and delighted with Boaz's
attention. She bows low to the ground. The text says she
"fell on her face" before him (see 2:10). In chapter 3, Boaz
is humbled and delighted by Ruth's attention. When she
arrives at the threshing floor, he is lying face down (see
3:8).

What other contrasts or similarities do you notice between chapters 2 and 3? These are not accidental. Boaz initiates the chapter 2 meeting; Ruth instigates the chapter 3 meeting. The discussion in chapter 2 occurs in the field; the meeting in chapter 3 takes place on a threshing floor. The first meeting is by day; the second, by night. The first is public; the second, private.

Both meetings are between two ordinary people who set up a sequence of events to achieve God's special intentions without knowing it.

THE SYMMETRY OF WINGS

The most wonderful symmetry of all is how Boaz and Ruth both talk about wings. In chapter 2, he blesses her for seeking refuge under the God of Israel's wings (see 2:12). In the full light of day, he says, in effect, "May you find refuge under the wings of God." Then at midnight, Ruth asks Boaz to spread his "wings" over her (see 3:9)! She takes the blanket off of his feet and asks him to cover her with it. Boaz eagerly agrees, and now Ruth is under her redeemer's wing, under his cover and protection, where she will remain for the rest of her life.

In ancient Hebrew, the words for "wings," "cover," and "blanket" are closely related. The word-pictures here are stunningly beautiful. The choice of this word shows us the skill and elegance of the storyteller. Oftentimes we think of the authors of the Bible as primitive and under-educated. It is true they did not learn science. But, we must admit, they are writing at genius levels of artistry and beauty.

As Ruth discovers, Boaz will also be her provider. Before and after their midnight meeting, he overloads her with food, bread, wine, and six measures of barley. In becoming her redeemer, Boaz will protect *and* provide for her. His is the generous heart of a loyal nobleman.

Hundreds of years later, there will be another, even more noble, a man born in Boaz's hometown, the little town of Bethlehem. He will eagerly take on the role of Redeemer, spreading his wings of protection and provision over us all.

～

God blesses and protects us through Jesus Christ.

～

THINKING MORE ABOUT IT

- How do you see Jesus in Boaz?
- How do you need to find "refuge under the wings of God?"
- Whose wings are you under? Who or what protects and provides for you?

18

WHAT MAKES A WORTHY WOMAN

". . . all my fellow townsmen know that you are a worthy woman."
RUTH 3:11

The books of the Christian Old Testament are part of the Hebrew Bible called the *Tanakh*. The word is an acronym for *Torah* ("Teaching," also known as the Five Books of Moses), *Nevi'im* ("Prophets"), and *Ketuvim* ("Writings")—hence, TaNaKh.

While Christians and Jews share the same list of books, the Old Testament and the Tanakh order them differently. For example, Ruth appears directly after Judges in our Old Testament, but the Tanakh places the Book of Ruth after the Wisdom writings, specifically right after the Book of Proverbs. Why? One reason could be that Proverbs ends with the famous description of the "Proverbs 31 woman," who Ruth embodies. Flipping between the Book of Ruth and Proverbs 31, the similarities are striking:

1. She is an exceptional woman.
2. She is loving and loyal to her mother-in-law.
3. All notice her excellent character.
4. She is described as "worth seven sons." That is a huge statement.
5. She overflows with *hesed*, as we have seen.
6. She takes care of her family.
7. She is beautiful.
8. She shows deep respect for her husband.
9. She is a hard worker, very diligent.

The only negative thing Ruth's contemporaries could say about her was that she was from an ethnic group out of favor with the Israelites. She was of the people who were the Israelites' dreaded enemies. She was of a different race, a separate and disdained ethnic group. But she was the model person who acted like a true Israelite at every turn. Ruth's choice to leave her people and go to Naomi's unknown land was nearly identical to the calling and migration of the first person ever to be called out by God —Abraham. He too went to a strange land.

Ruth followed in the footsteps of Father Abraham, who would one day also be the father of her faith. She might have been on the outside of the faith, but she acted like a true believer.

Jesus once told a group of proud Pharisees the story about the Good Samaritan. He made the same point about real virtue. Ruth and the Good Samaritan embody the same noble values. This is one of the great lessons from the Book of Ruth that is applicable in our time. As we see from this story written nearly 3,200 years ago, the Bible is consistent with the idea that Martin Luther King, Jr., spoke in our day; that we should be judged not by our skin color but by the content of our character.

THE GRACE OF GLEANING

Earlier we quoted the great statement of St. Augustine. "The Old Testament is the New Testament concealed, The New Testament is the Old Testament revealed". We can unpack this idea here.

Augustine meant that the Old Testament is filled with allusions, illustrations, and ideas that point forward to the time and the storyline of the New Testament. Stories in the Old Testament sometimes suggest something that cannot be fully known or understood until it is revealed in the pages of the New Testament and the work of Jesus Christ.

For example, the story of Ruth occurs during the harvest when all the people in the little town of Bethlehem are gathering the rich stores of grain for the coming year. This grain will become their bread. But now, try to think theologically about what a harvest really is and the lessons that Ruth learns as she gleans.

We know that harvesting comes at the end of a long process of turning soil, tossing seeds, tending shoots, and watching temperatures and seasons change. In other words, for all her industry and initiative, Ruth, was the beneficiary of someone else's work. She was thankful, but she was not proud to have done it all—she didn't. Ruth was humbled that there was so much, but she could not be proud to have made it all happen.

Ruth exemplifies how future generations will come to understand the Grace of God—that it is unmerited favor from our loving and generous God.

This short but powerful story tells us something that the New Testament will thoroughly explain. Our Lord Jesus blesses us with His finished work on the Cross. This work is provided for our salvation; we did not contribute to it. We did not earn it. We have not warranted it. But it is ours nonetheless, and, like Ruth, we should make every effort to procure it for ourselves and others, always with a thankful and humble heart.

∼

God honors those who show others simple human kindness.

∼

THINKING MORE ABOUT IT

- How do you see Ruth's behavior as a picture of unmerited favor and grace?

- Why doesn't it matter to God where you come from?
- Which of Ruth's many virtues stand out to you? Why?

<u>Deeper Dive</u>: Read Proverbs 31 and Luke 10:25–37.

19

THE FAMILY

*"But if he is not willing to redeem you, then, as
the LORD lives, I will redeem you."*
RUTH 3:13

W e've looked from different angles at a powerful truth hiding in plain sight in Ruth's story: that God uses people, even messy people whose lives are imperfect or broken, to work His will in the world. Most of us see this as good news because it means He can use even the likes of you and me.

But there is another truth, perhaps just as powerful, woven seamlessly into Ruth's story—a truth about something that is as messy, imperfect, and broken as our individual lives. Namely, that God uses families

The Book of Ruth is an over-the-top, unbelievably posi-
tive endorsement of the family and its benefits for
humans individually and humanity overall. In the early
verses, a family of four's prospects weigh them down. Life
is hard and then turns deadly. However, there is another
family of four in the closing verses, and their opportuni-
ties lift them! Life has been challenging, but God has
redeemed it all. And between the opening and closing
vignettes, we find faithful family love (*hesed*) between
Naomi and Ruth, the duty of a relative to help out a
family member, and the head of a new family (Boaz)
providing for his new wife, mother-in-law, and son.

It is a marvelous thing to think about. Boaz, by acting
with redemptive *hesed*, creates one of the most important
families in the Bible. By his initiative, he made a family
that did three things: protected Ruth, provided for
Naomi, and produced a son named Obed. This is brilliant!

THE LITTLE CHURCH

Pope John Paul II once referred to the family as an *eccle-
siola* or "little church."[1*] It is the place where children are
welcomed, protected, nurtured, and raised into adult-
hood. It is the place where husband and wife can care for
one another, face life's inevitable challenges together, give
mutual support during losses, and enjoy the intimacy of
lifelong love. It is the primary vehicle for the transmission
of biblical faith to a new generation. That is "church" at its
very best.

The family was God's first "aftermarket" creation. As the earliest story in Genesis shows us, God created the entire world and everything in it. The text describes the ordering of nothingness and chaos into the good and beautiful creation that surrounds us and includes us. Then He rested.

But then He decided to make one more thing (see Genesis 2:18–25). Families are just that important. They are so important that Jesus created a new one *from the Cross*. Even as he was dying, he provided for his mother's care and protection. He gave her as a mother to the apostle John and gave John to her as a son (see John 19:26–27).

Most families are messy. All are far from perfect. Quite often, the best of them are made of people just trying to do their best for each other in the face of the hard realities of life.

Consider the Holy Family, whose story Christians tell and retell every Christmas Eve. Looking from the outside, Joseph and Mary were barely making it. They were both on the move. He had left his employment. She was a pregnant teen. They were all but homeless.

In other words, Jesus was born into the most precarious yet precious of human arrangements: the family. God knew what He was doing when he placed His Son there to be tenderly cared for, nurtured, raised, taught, and then sent on His mission.

God does not use only so called "nuclear families" that consist of a husband, wife, and children. After all, in the

Book of Ruth, the nuclear family in the first chapter is brought to its knees. But by God's good grace, He causes another, more patchwork, family to come together: a widowed mother and her widowed daughter-in-law who marries the mother's much older relative. When the twice-married woman from a foreign and forbidden country gives birth to a baby boy, the older mother becomes both a matriarch and a nursemaid—and the baby, Obed, becomes a branch in the Messiah's family tree. Who would have thought a family so "messy" would be in our Lord's family tree?

∿

God's way creates, supports, upholds, and protects the ordinary family.

∿

THINKING MORE ABOUT IT

- How is God at work in your family?
- How is your family like a "little church?"
- How could your family reach out to your neighbors?

20

NO SECRETS

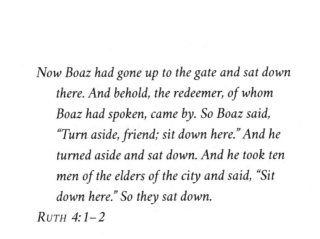

Now Boaz had gone up to the gate and sat down
there. And behold, the redeemer, of whom
Boaz had spoken, came by. So Boaz said,
"Turn aside, friend; sit down here." And he
turned aside and sat down. And he took ten
men of the elders of the city and said, "Sit
down here." So they sat down.

RUTH 4:1–2

D o you notice how much sitting happens in the first couple verses of Ruth chapter 4? Five times in just two verses, somebody sits down. First Boaz, then the unnamed potential redeemer, then ten members of the city council—they all sit down to get in on the action.

Why all this sitting down?

First, they need to stay put to do their business. All parties and witnesses must be present and attentive. There's a formality to it. Twelve men are seated at the city gate for the duration of negotiations. An offer is made to Elimelech's closer unnamed relative. He considers it, does his "due diligence," and then declines. Now Boaz has an opportunity to take responsibility for redemption. The text explains an ancient Israelite custom involving a sandal exchange to serve as a surety bond for their agreement.

Second, the two men negotiate publicly in the presence of elders. They do not do their deal in secret. There is no plotting or conniving. Boaz clarifies that he wants to be Ruth's redeemer, showing the community's leaders that he will bear the burden without reluctance or hesitation. Boaz is taking a significant risk—remember, Ruth has not yet shown herself capable of producing children. If he redeems the land and marries Ruth and proves to be infertile, she will still be his responsibility. Yes, Boaz does all of this publicly. He does not give himself an "out." And by conducting his business out in the open, he shows us that he holds his heart's desire, Ruth, with an open hand. If their union is God's will, then God will make a way.

All the witnesses, sitting still to see redemption in action, are delighted and express their well-wishes and superlatives for prosperity and fecundity.

IN THE OPEN FOR ALL TO SEE

Everything is done decently, in order, and in the full light of day.

Transparency is one of the hallmarks of biblical faith. There are no secret codes, esoteric knowledge, or hidden features that are only disclosed to the favored few. One of the most pernicious of all heresies is Gnosticism, the idea that there is unique insight or knowledge given only to some, to the elect, the chosen, who must keep the precious secret from everyone else. This is not so; it has never been so.

The magnificent and marvelous things of God are done in the full light of day, not in a dark corner.

The Gospel is not secret knowledge or hidden revelations available only to a few. The Bible is not a codebook unlocking an ancient mystery to those "on the inside." Instead, God does the extraordinary when we commit ourselves to what attorneys call "full disclosure." When we have nothing to hide, God's will can shine forth.

Consider one more thing about this sit-down meeting at the city gate. Boaz makes public his commitment to protect Ruth and provide for Naomi. Imagine how Ruth and Naomi felt when Boaz stood up and placed them under his wing. Joy? Undoubtedly. Relief? For sure. Were they amazed at what God had brought about? Yes, and more. Ruth and Naomi must have realized that the God of Abraham, Isaac, and Jacob was good.

The emotion in this scene is powerful. The deep sense of joy, relief, love, and thankfulness that all of these characters feel reminds me of the famous quote from Ralph Waldo Emerson's ode to success. The last line of his poem might perfectly describe the success that Boaz achieved in his life. "To know even one life has breathed easier because you have lived. This is to have succeeded."

～

There are many unknowns with God, but there are no secrets.

～

THINKING MORE ABOUT IT

What stands out in this chapter to you?

Do you see the Bible as transparent?

How encouraging is it to know that the Gospel is not a hidden secret?

A KINSMAN REDEEMER

*Then he said to the redeemer, "Naomi, who has
come back from the country of Moab, is
selling the parcel of land that belonged to our
relative Elimelech."*
RUTH 4:3

At the heart of the Book of Ruth is the need for a
redeemer. The word for *redeem, buy,* or *purchase*
is used 23 times in the story, 15 times in the
last chapter alone.

The word means "to set free by paying the price." In effect,
redemption is a reversal, whether out of a bad situation, a
lost cause, or a dead end. But the key to every redemption
story is that someone must pay the price; a sacrifice must
be made. In Ruth and Naomi's case, the rights to Elimelech's land passed to Ruth's husband, Mahlon, when

Elimelech died. But Mahlon had also perished in Moab, and, as women, neither Ruth nor Naomi can carry the title in her name. Even more to the point, the land is under some kind of lien or mortgage, and they are too poor to redeem it from the creditors.

In Israel during this time, land cannot be bought or sold. It is an inheritance from the Lord God; it is not for sale. However, if family fortunes turn south, the land can be leveraged, leased, or otherwise encumbered for the family's survival. But as with most debts, it becomes harder and harder over time to pay back the loan and redeem the land out of its encumbrance.

This is Naomi's situation. She is in hock. She owes a debt she cannot pay. And even if she could settle the debt, she will face another problem: She has no male heir. Her sons have died, and she has only her daughter-in-law left. (Anyone in the ancient world who heard this story would see this "redemption problem" right away.)

There is a way to manage the redemption problem. The closest relative to the indebted landowner can step in and settle the debt. In fact, in most cases, he is *required* to do so. Such a relative is known as a kinsman-redeemer; the Hebrew word is *go'el*. Two things have to be true for such a person to redeem the land. First, he needs to be close enough in blood to be considered a member of that family. Second, he must have the means to pay the debt to save the land from being lost to the family forever.

NEED A REDEEMER

Boaz agrees to redeem the land—and with it, Ruth and Naomi—but one legality has to be addressed first. Another family member is "closer" than Boaz and therefore has first dibs on settling the debt and claiming the land. After consideration, however, he turns it down. He is not willing to pay the price.

The word *redemption* perfectly describes the story of the Bible. It is hinted at as early as Genesis 3:15, when God tells the serpent that someone from Eve's lineage will come to crush his head, paying the price of a bruised heel. And through to the last book of the Bible, it is the Lord Jesus who is hailed as our Redeemer; He is the one who paid our ransom.

The Book of Ruth is not just a remarkable story. For that matter, it is not only a demonstration of God's sovereignty. There is a real, life-or-death predicament at the heart of the story. Unless there is outside help from someone who is also on the inside—a redeemer—things will not turn out right.

But of course, help is on the way. It comes in the form of an ordinary man. Boaz freely pays for the land and for Ruth, even though he is under no obligation or requirement. As we have seen all along, our extraordinary God uses ordinary people to make extraordinary things happen.

The Book of Ruth is a mini-gospel all by itself, foreshadowing this turn of phrase: "He paid a debt he did not owe;

we owed a debt we could not pay." Christ paid our debt to make us free and set things right. He was human as we are, our kinsman. But he came with God's means to pay our debt.

He is the Redeemer we need. He is willing and able still.

~

God is willing and able to be our Redeemer.

~

THINKING MORE ABOUT IT

- Do you need to be set free? Do you have a debt you can't pay?
- What would it feel like to be debt free?
- What has Jesus redeemed?

2 2

UNPRAYED PRAYERS

Then Naomi took the child and laid him on her
lap, and became his nurse. And the women of
the neighborhood gave him a name, saying,
"A son has been born to Naomi." They named
him Obed. He was the father of Jesse, the
father of David.
RUTH 4:16–17

N o one prays in the Book of Ruth. There are no recorded petitions, intercessions, confessions, or direct appeals to God. This is not an oversight, I believe, but an important lesson deliberately conveyed: that good can happen to us and in us even if we never think to pray about it. Let me explain.

There are three kinds of prayers. We know about the *answered* and *unanswered* varieties, but there is also a third kind: prayers we do not pray. We don't even know to pray them. They are longings deep within us—hopes, wishes, or dreams that are too wild or impossible to ever speak before God.

Naomi receives two answers for the prayers she never prays.

Remember in the early part of the story when Naomi hopes for two things? I use the word "hopes" instead of "prays" because she expresses them not to God but to her daughters-in-law. Her first hope is that each of the young widows will find rest in the home of a new husband (see Ruth 1:9). Her second hope is that, somehow, she might have more sons. She expresses her longing as an impossible, almost absurd, dream: "Have I yet sons in my womb that they may become your husbands?" (Ruth 1:11).

She's not serious, of course. She is old, and her womb is barren. And besides, she doesn't even have a husband. This is more like a wish than a prayer.

PRAYERS THAT ARE UNPRAYED

And yet, God answers both of Naomi's unprayed prayers. The first is answered when Ruth tells her about Boaz's kind attentions in his field, and Naomi sees the glimmer of a chance to settle Ruth in the home of a new husband. We can imagine the older widow exclaiming, "I never saw it coming!" This is God's answer to an unprayed prayer.

Through the dynamic miracle of human will and divine action, God then answers Naomi's second unprayed prayer. Ruth and Boaz marry and produce baby Obed (the couple does the work, as it were, but the story says God "gave conception" to Ruth). Naomi now has the son she could not have even imagined praying to receive!

She places the boy on her lap and becomes his nurse.

Naomi had left Moab empty, but God uses Ruth, Boaz, harvesters, romance, Levitical Law, and someone else's marriage to provide her a baby so close to being her own that the village women call him *her* son. She had dreamed an impossible dream, and it came to be. Naomi is called a mother to baby Obed.

We all have unanswered prayers. Prayer can be frustrating and sometimes feel pointless. Most of us keep praying anyway because, now and then, we receive a clear, visible answer. But we have so many more that remain unanswered. What are we to do?

Naomi, with Obed on her lap, has some counsel for us, I think. She would tell us to start counting answers to our *unprayed* prayers. That is, to open our eyes and see the good things God has given us without our even asking, to see the blessings God has bestowed on us when we didn't know what we wanted. If we are alive today, it is because God has given us what we needed to survive, often without our conscious awareness. He just blesses us.

No one prays in the Book of Ruth, but everyone is the beneficiary of an overflow of God's *hesed*, his abundant love. He answers prayers we didn't even know to pray.

~

God provides for our needs even though we may not dream to ask.

~

THINKING MORE ABOUT IT

- What are things you have received that you never thought to pray for?
- Is it comforting to know that God answers even when we don't even know to pray?
- What do you think about Naomi's practical advice for us today?

23

RACE AND MARRIAGE

So Boaz took Ruth, and she became his wife. And
he went in to her, and the LORD gave her
conception, and she bore a son.
RUTH 4:13

Boaz and Ruth are hardly the picture-perfect couple. A wide age difference separates them. They don't know each other very well. Their marriage is sudden. They are from two different cultures and lands. And there's another evident and visible disparity: They are of two different races and religions.

Boaz is an Israelite; Ruth, a Moabite. Boaz has been instructed in the Law, and the Law warns against marriage across ethnic lines, particularly when it comes to the Moabites. They are a cursed ethnic group whose descendants are barred from any assembly of the Lord for ten generations (see Deuteronomy 23:3–6). The Israelites worship the God of Abraham, Isaac, and Jacob, while the Moabites worship a god named Chemosh, whose priests preside over child sacrifices. It is not hard to see why Israelites are warned against having anything to do with them.

And yet Boaz the Israelite and Ruth the Moabitess cross racial lines and are married, and their descendants are in the line of the future King David and Mary, the mother of Jesus.

Is their marriage legal? Does God permit interracial marriage?

Remember that Ruth's pledge to Naomi includes a heartfelt commitment to leave the Moabites' god and cleave to Naomi and her God. "Your people shall be my people, and your God my God" (Ruth 1:16). Ruth binds herself to Naomi by a confession to the God of Abraham, Isaac, and Jacob.

In other words, Ruth becomes a Jew. She may be a Moabite by origin, but she leaves all that behind when she and Naomi set out for Bethlehem. And even though she is regarded as a Moabitess, Ruth does not see herself as such. Remember, she asks Boaz to be her kinsman-redeemer. She sees herself as a Jew, subject to Jewish laws, customs, and traditions.

Boaz does not marry a follower of Chemosh; he marries a follower of the one true God.

In my youth, interracial marriage was a subject for hushed

tones around the dinner table. The older generation in my household had a very simple idea about it: Don't do it. It was not to be done. I can't remember what sources were cited for its prohibition, but undoubtedly someone made the appeal to the Bible. "The Bible is against it!", I am sure was said more than once.

But, the Bible provides for it; the Bible allows interracial marriage. Moses married a dark-skinned Ethiopian woman, a Cushite, and God was angry that Moses' siblings, Aaron and Miriam, were critical of the relationship (see Numbers 12). The Israelites were forbidden from marrying Canaanites and other pagan people, but this prohibition was based on their foreign faith and religious practices, not their race or ethnicity. In the New Testament, the only reason Paul gave to discourage two people from marrying was if one was an unbeliever (see 2 Corinthians 6:14).

Ruth's story is not as simple or straightforward as it appears. Layers of history and theology are threaded through the story, and the Book of Ruth challenged a lot of the cultural assumptions and prejudices embedded in those layers. And thus, the Book of Ruth should cause us to examine our biases and assumptions today.

It seems that the Book of Ruth and the teaching of the Bible has some shocking news for my parents and their dinner party conversations. Namely, that people should marry based on a shared faith, not a shared race.

~

God builds communities of people by faith, not race.

◡

THINKING MORE ABOUT IT

- Can you imagine the challenges that Boaz and Ruth face in their marriage?
- Do different backgrounds cause difficulty in your relationships?
- How important was the foundation of their similar belief in God?

24

REDEEMED, THEN RESTORED

*He shall be to you a restorer of life and a
nourisher of your old age, for your daughter-
in-law who loves you, who is more to you
than seven sons, has given birth to him.*
RUTH 4:15

L et us come back to Naomi for a minute. If we
shine a spotlight on the supporting actress's role
in this amazing book, we see a remarkable
series of events that show us God's restorative work.
Naomi's journey from joy to sadness and back again may
be a subplot, but it can encourage anyone who has faced
darkness, grief, or loss or who may feel lost even now.

The women of Bethlehem can't believe their eyes when
Naomi comes home from Moab. "Is this Naomi?" they ask

(see Ruth 1:19). Her ten-year extended stay in the country to the east has left a mark; her face tells the tale.

But later, Naomi once again becomes the talk of the town —only this time, the women give praise to God for Ruth's son: *"A son has been born to Naomi"* (Ruth 4:16). They know who gave birth to Obed, but they're not wrong. They know what has happened. Naomi has been redeemed *and* restored.

> *"Blessed be the LORD, who has not left you this day without a redeemer, and may his name be renowned in Israel! He shall be to you a restorer of life and a nourisher of your old age, for your daughter-in-law who loves you, who is more to you than seven sons, has given birth to him"* (Ruth 4:14–15).

Do you see the two gifts God gives to Naomi? Boaz redeems her, and Obed restores her. Boaz pays for the past; Obed is a down payment on the future.

R AND R

These are the gifts all Christian believers receive through Jesus Christ. Redemption focuses on our past; restoration has our future in mind.

This is New Testament language, too; it is how Jesus worked in his healing ministry. Remember when the four men brought their paralyzed friend to the house where Jesus was teaching in Capernaum? (See Mark 2:1–12.) They created an opening in the roof and lowered their friend's bed so that he was lying directly in front of Jesus.

Jesus had two things to say to the paralyzed man. First, Jesus told him that He had forgiven his sins. That is *redemption*. Then Jesus restored the use of his legs. "That you may know that the Son of Man has authority on earth to forgive sins . . . I say to you, rise, pick up your bed, and go home" (Mark 2:10–11). That is *restoration*.

If we think of the Bible as a four-act play, we can see how restoration is the final point and promise of the narrative itself. First is *Creation*, followed quickly by the *Fall*. Most of the rest centers on the search for someone to set things right again, for *Redemption*. The past must be atoned. It must be redeemed.

But that is not the end of the story. There is one more act: The created order must be restored. *Restoration* is the final act, and the grand finale brings glory to God.

Naomi's life is a miniature version of this grand four-act play.

∼

God not only redeems our past; He restores us for our future.

∼

THINKING MORE ABOUT IT

Can you see the difference between being redeemed and being restored?

How encouraging is it that Naomi is not only redeemed but restored?

In what ways has God restored your life?

25

THE GOSPEL FROM RUTH

Now these are the generations of Perez: Perez
fathered Hezron, Hezron fathered Ram, Ram
fathered Amminadab, Amminadab fathered
Nahshon, Nahshon fathered Salmon, Salmon
fathered Boaz, Boaz fathered Obed, Obed
fathered Jesse, Jesse fathered David.
RUTH *4:18–22*

S everal Old Testament books include a genealogy of some kind; often, they begin with it or wedge it into the middle of the narrative. Readers are understandably tempted to race over a long list of names, thinking it unimportant. But the genealogy found in the Book of Ruth—one of the shortest in Scripture—should be carefully considered. This list of names is the key to one of the core themes in this remarkable little book.

The list of names begins with Perez (4:18), which ties the events of Ruth's story to the patriarchs, to the generation after Jacob. (If Boaz's mother, Rahab, was a bit of a black sheep in the family line, she wasn't the only one!) Let's go back just a bit to the history of the patriarchs.

Abraham had two children: Ishmael and Isaac. Isaac had two children, Esau and Jacob. In a culture where being "firstborn" meant everything, birth order was a vital statistic. When Jacob and Esau were born, there was a tussle between the firstborn (Esau) and his fraternal twin, Jacob, who was born holding tight to his brother's heel. In the next generation, there was a conception and birthing contest between Jacob's wives and concubines. The last son born to his first wife, Leah, was named Judah.

In time, Judah grew up and had several sons, one of whom was named Er. Judah chose Tamar to be Er's wife. The Bible says God disliked Er, however, and put him to death! Then Judah told a younger son, Onan, to marry his brother's widow (this was standard practice), but Onan didn't want to have children with her. After years of *coitus interruptus,* God put Onan to death, too. Judah decided not to risk any more sons; it would be best for Tamar to remain a widow and never have children. But Tamar took matters into her own hands. She tricked her father-in-law into a clandestine session in a tent and conceived twins.

Later, when Tamar's twins were born, one of their hands emerged from the birth canal, and the attending midwife tied a scarlet ribbon around his wrist to mark the first-born. The other child held the firstborn back, however, and came through the birth canal first. He was named Perez, which means "breakthrough" or "breach."

That is the colorful story behind the first-named patriarch in Boaz's family tree.

The point of this family history is to show the inscrutable ways of God. Boaz, Rahab's son, and Perez's great-great-great-grandchild marries a member of the Moabite race. And then together, these two unlikely people conceive a child who, in time, will become great-grandfather to David, who will be king.

In this way, the Book of Ruth is a hinge. It swings from the old patriarchy of betrayal, deception, and dysfunction on one side to bring redemption and family restoration on the other. God doesn't overlook the sins and transgressions of the past; he uses them to reveal the coming of a future king who will set all things right and rule over all things rightly. A king is coming—even if the world must wait for another child to be born in Bethlehem centuries later.

In other words, the Book of Ruth is a Gospel. It heralds the good news to come. Her story begins with the worst of all verdicts: a broken government without just rulers, a terrible famine afflicting God's chosen people, and three tragic deaths. But it ends looking toward the horizon of a righteous government led by King David, a bountiful harvest that supplies bread for the hungry, and—instead of funerals—a wedding and the birth of a new son.

God's way is to use ordinary people to prepare the way of the Lord.

∼

THINKING MORE ABOUT IT

- How does your lineage, your family tree, compare to Ruth's?
- Can you see a course of redemption in your family's story?
- Has the Book of Ruth changed how you see the ordinary things in your life?

Deeper Dive: Re-read the Book of Ruth and write your plotline synopsis.

∼

EPILOGUE

I hope that reading the Book of Ruth has been good for your soul. You may have become fascinated by the plot and the people; I did. It feels like a story for our time. It begins with sadness and loss but ends with hope and promise, and in between is a full range of human emotions that resonates deeply even in our modern lives. I trust that the characters we've met together are now real, historical, three-dimensional people for you. Their actions and choices link directly to the New Testament's message and the work of Jesus on the Cross; I hope I have illuminated those links.

But remember that the Book of Ruth is about ordinary people who lived through tragedy, loss, migration, uncertainty, and love. The plot is not particularly extraordinary; it's a typical human saga of hardship, adventure, hope, and promise. And the people in the story are, by themselves, unremarkable—except, perhaps, for the courage with which they face their troubling circumstances.

I have tried to show that our majestic, holy, extraordinary God does move within the ordinary framework of humanity and human lives. Working through regular people's lives is God's M.O.—that is, His *modus operandi,* His way of operating. Working in and through the daily lives of people doing ordinary things is the ordinary way of God.

Most readers of the Old and New Testaments find that the more they study, the deeper their studies take them. Everywhere they look, there are hints, types, and shadows of the Gospel. We find inexhaustible treasures everywhere in the Bible, in any book we carefully examine. Please do not think God's ordinary ways are confined to the days of the Bible or relegated to only a select few. If you read the Scriptures closely and ask the Holy Spirit for insights and understanding, you will discover why this book of books is endlessly fascinating and wonderfully enriching.

I pray you will find your own life to be the perfect place for our loving God to use you as an instrument for His greater purpose. Using you and using me, such as we are —these are the ordinary ways of God.

The Rev. Canon David Roseberry

2021

AFTERWORD

You may be wondering about the process I use to study the Scriptures. Here is a quick look at how I, as the old Anglican prayer says, "read, mark, learn, and inwardly digest the truth of God's word."

Do you remember English literature class in high school? Do you remember receiving dreaded weekend homework assignments to read and decipher a poem by Tennyson, Yeats, or e. e. cummings? For me, poetry was never easy. The lyrics seemed opaque; I would often wonder why the poet didn't just come out and say in plain English what he was thinking.

When I attended college, I had similar assignments but improved with each semester. It was there that I first heard the term "close reading" as it applies to the study of complex poetry and essays. A close reading is a slow, strategic, and careful read-through of an assigned text. Years later, in seminary, I received the same assignments from my biblical studies and preaching professors, only they called it "exegesis." Exegesis, the study of how a biblical text relates to the writer's culture and the rest of the Bible, is a standard and weekly practice for all preachers and teachers of Scripture.

Today some might use more descriptive words to describe this process. They might call it a "deep dive," for example. I like that. As I see it, diving deep is what I do. Over my years of ministry, taking a deep dive into the biblical text has become my favorite part of preparing a sermon.

When we read books of the Bible like ancient novellas or short historical narrative, poetry, history, or ancient wisdom—the Bible contains all of these—we discover many wonderful truths. But if we *slow down* our reading (maybe even reading out loud!), looking closely and deliberately at the text and diving into the details, we find even greater treasures. When we dive deep into the text, context, clues, words, phrases, connections, metaphors, and structure, we uncover ever more beauty and truth. The deeper we go, the brighter it gets!

Ultimately, as has happened to countless readers of the Bible, we find ourselves in a world of hope and wonder, joy and love. Every study session ends with thanksgiving and praise of our holy and infinitely good God.

A NOTE FROM THE PUBLISHER

~

Have you enjoyed, "The Ordinary Ways of God"? If so, please find other books listed at the RMLBooks Website. Go to LeaderWorks.org/books

Also, it would help if you would leave a review on Amazon.

NOTES

13. ORDINARY PEOPLE

1. *Oswald Chambers, *My Utmost for His Highest*, "Submitting to God's Purpose" (October 25), https://utmost.org/submitting-to-god%e2%80%99s-purpose/ (accessed January 2021).

14. THE BIGGEST WORD IN THE WORLD

1. *(While Ruth has no power of her own, she does represent Boaz's future legacy. And she submits herself to him for *his* greater good.)

15. OUR REDEEMER RELATIVE

1. *See chapter 11 and the quote from Ephesians 2.

19. THE FAMILY

1. *John Paul II, "Intervention in the Sistine Chapel, DELIVERED, 6 Council Episcoporum," September 26, 1980. http://www.vatican.va/content/john-paul-ii/la/homilies/1980/documents/hf_jp-ii_hom_19800926_sinodo.html (accessed January 2020).

THE BOOK OF RUTH

THE KING JAMES VERSION

CHAPTER ONE

Now it came to pass in the days when the judges ruled, that there was a famine in the land. And a certain man of Bethlehemjudah went to sojourn in the country of Moab, he, and his wife, and his two sons.

2 And the name of the man was Elimelech, and the name of his wife Naomi, and the name of his two sons Mahlon and Chilion, Ephrathites of Bethlehem judah. And they came into the country of Moab, and continued there.

3 And Elimelech Naomi's husband died; and she was left, and her two sons.

4 And they took them wives of the women of Moab; the name of the one was Orpah, and the name of the other Ruth: and they dwelled there about ten years.

5 And Mahlon and Chilion died also both of them; and the woman was left of her two sons and her husband.

6 Then she arose with her daughters in law, that she might return from the country of Moab: for she had heard in the country of Moab how that the Lord had visited his people in giving them bread.

7 Wherefore she went forth out of the place where she was, and her two daughters in law with her; and they went on the way to return unto the land of Judah.

8 And Naomi said unto her two daughters in law, Go, return each to her mother's house: the Lord deal kindly with you, as ye have dealt with the dead, and with me.

9 The Lord grant you that ye may find rest, each of you in the house of her husband. Then she kissed them; and they lifted up their voice, and wept.

10 And they said unto her, Surely we will return with thee unto thy people.

11 And Naomi said, Turn again, my daughters: why will ye go with me? are there yet any more sons in my womb, that they may be your husbands?

12 Turn again, my daughters, go your way; for I am too old to have an husband. If I should say, I have hope, if I should have an husband also to night, and should also bear sons;

13 Would ye tarry for them till they were grown? would ye stay for them from having husbands? nay, my daughters; for it grieveth me much for your sakes that the hand of the Lord is gone out against me.

14 And they lifted up their voice, and wept again: and Orpah kissed her mother in law; but Ruth clave unto her.

15 And she said, Behold, thy sister in law is gone back unto her people, and unto her gods: return thou after thy sister in law.

16 And Ruth said, Intreat me not to leave thee, or to return from following after thee: for whither thou goest, I will go; and where thou lodgest, I will lodge: thy people shall be my people, and thy God my God:

17 Where thou diest, will I die, and there will I be buried: the Lord do so to me, and more also, if ought but death part thee and me.

18 When she saw that she was stedfastly minded to go with her, then she left speaking unto her.

19 So they two went until they came to Bethlehem. And it came to pass, when they were come to Bethlehem, that all the city was moved about them, and they said, Is this Naomi?

20 And she said unto them, Call me not Naomi, call me Mara: for the Almighty hath dealt very bitterly with me.

21 I went out full and the Lord hath brought me home again empty: why then call ye me Naomi, seeing the Lord hath testified against me, and the Almighty hath afflicted me?

22 So Naomi returned, and Ruth the Moabitess, her daughter in law, with her, which returned out of the country of Moab: and they came to Bethlehem in the beginning of barley harvest.

CHAPTER TWO

And Naomi had a kinsman of her husband's, a mighty man of wealth, of the family of Elimelech; and his name was Boaz.

2 And Ruth the Moabitess said unto Naomi, Let me now go to the field, and glean ears of corn after him in whose sight I shall find grace. And she said unto her, Go, my daughter.

3 And she went, and came, and gleaned in the field after the reapers: and her hap was to light on a part of the field belonging unto Boaz, who was of the kindred of Elimelech.

4 And, behold, Boaz came from Bethlehem, and said unto the reapers, The Lord be with you. And they answered him, The Lord bless thee.

5 Then said Boaz unto his servant that was set over the reapers, Whose damsel is this?

6 And the servant that was set over the reapers answered and said, It is the Moabitish damsel that came back with Naomi out of the country of Moab:

7 And she said, I pray you, let me glean and gather after the reapers among the sheaves: so she came, and hath continued even from the morning until now, that she tarried a little in the house.

8 Then said Boaz unto Ruth, Hearest thou not, my daughter? Go not to glean in another field, neither go from hence, but abide here fast by my maidens:

9 Let thine eyes be on the field that they do reap, and go thou after them: have I not charged the young men that they shall not touch thee? and when thou art athirst, go unto the vessels, and drink of that which the young men have drawn.

10 Then she fell on her face, and bowed herself to the ground, and said unto him, Why have I found grace in thine eyes, that thou shouldest take knowledge of me, seeing I am a stranger?

11 And Boaz answered and said unto her, It hath fully been shewed me, all that thou hast done unto thy mother in law since the death of thine husband: and how thou hast left thy father and thy mother, and the land of thy nativity, and art come unto a people which thou knewest not heretofore.

12 The Lord recompense thy work, and a full reward be given thee of the Lord God of Israel, under whose wings thou art come to trust.

13 Then she said, Let me find favour in thy sight, my lord; for that thou hast comforted me, and for that thou hast spoken friendly unto thine handmaid, though I be not like unto one of thine handmaidens.

14 And Boaz said unto her, At mealtime come thou hither, and eat of the bread, and dip thy morsel in the vinegar.

And she sat beside the reapers: and he reached her parched corn, and she did eat, and was sufficed, and left.

15 And when she was risen up to glean, Boaz commanded his young men, saying, Let her glean even among the sheaves, and reproach her not:

16 And let fall also some of the handfuls of purpose for her, and leave them, that she may glean them, and rebuke her not.

17 So she gleaned in the field until even, and beat out that she had gleaned: and it was about an ephah of barley.

18 And she took it up, and went into the city: and her mother in law saw what she had gleaned: and she brought forth, and gave to her that she had reserved after she was sufficed.

19 And her mother in law said unto her, Where hast thou gleaned to day? and where wroughtest thou? blessed be he that did take knowledge of thee. And she shewed her mother in law with whom she had wrought, and said, The man's name with whom I wrought to day is Boaz.

20 And Naomi said unto her daughter in law, Blessed be he of the Lord, who hath not left off his kindness to the living and to the dead. And Naomi said unto her, The man is near of kin unto us, one of our next kinsmen.

21 And Ruth the Moabitess said, He said unto me also, Thou shalt keep fast by my young men, until they have ended all my harvest.

22 And Naomi said unto Ruth her daughter in law, It is good, my daughter, that thou go out with his maidens, that they meet thee not in any other field.

23 So she kept fast by the maidens of Boaz to glean unto the end of barley harvest and of wheat harvest; and dwelt with her mother in law.

CHAPTER THREE

Then Naomi her mother in law said unto her, My daughter, shall I not seek rest for thee, that it may be well with thee?

2 And now is not Boaz of our kindred, with whose maidens thou wast? Behold, he winnoweth barley to night in the threshingfloor.

3 Wash thyself therefore, and anoint thee, and put thy raiment upon thee, and get thee down to the floor: but make not thyself known unto the man, until he shall have done eating and drinking.

4 And it shall be, when he lieth down, that thou shalt mark the place where he shall lie, and thou shalt go in, and uncover his feet, and lay thee down; and he will tell thee what thou shalt do.

5 And she said unto her, All that thou sayest unto me I will do.

6 And she went down unto the floor, and did according to all that her mother in law bade her.

7 And when Boaz had eaten and drunk, and his heart was merry, he went to lie down at the end of the heap of corn: and she came softly, and uncovered his feet, and laid her down.

8 And it came to pass at midnight, that the man was afraid, and turned himself: and, behold, a woman lay at his feet.

9 And he said, Who art thou? And she answered, I am Ruth thine handmaid: spread therefore thy skirt over thine handmaid; for thou art a near kinsman.

10 And he said, Blessed be thou of the Lord, my daughter: for thou hast shewed more kindness in the latter end than at the beginning, inasmuch as thou followedst not young men, whether poor or rich.

11 And now, my daughter, fear not; I will do to thee all that thou requirest: for all the city of my people doth know that thou art a virtuous woman.

12 And now it is true that I am thy near kinsman: howbeit there is a kinsman nearer than I.

13 Tarry this night, and it shall be in the morning, that if he will perform unto thee the part of a kinsman, well; let him do the kinsman's part: but if he will not do the part of a kinsman to thee, then will I do the part of a kinsman to thee, as the Lord liveth: lie down until the morning.

14 And she lay at his feet until the morning: and she rose up before one could know another. And he said, Let it not be known that a woman came into the floor.

15 Also he said, Bring the vail that thou hast upon thee, and hold it. And when she held it, he measured six measures of barley, and laid it on her: and she went into the city.

16 And when she came to her mother in law, she said, Who art thou, my daughter? And she told her all that the man had done to her.

17 And she said, These six measures of barley gave he me; for he said to me, Go not empty unto thy mother in law.

18 Then said she, Sit still, my daughter, until thou know how the matter will fall: for the man will not be in rest, until he have finished the thing this day.

CHAPTER FOUR

Then went Boaz up to the gate, and sat him down there: and, behold, the kinsman of whom Boaz spake came by; unto whom he said, Ho, such a one! turn aside, sit down here. And he turned aside, and sat down.

2 And he took ten men of the elders of the city, and said, Sit ye down here. And they sat down.

3 And he said unto the kinsman, Naomi, that is come again out of the country of Moab, selleth a parcel of land, which was our brother Elimelech's:

4 And I thought to advertise thee, saying, Buy it before the inhabitants, and before the elders of my people. If thou wilt redeem it, redeem it: but if thou wilt not redeem it, then tell me, that I may know: for there is none to redeem it beside thee; and I am after thee. And he said, I will redeem it.

5 Then said Boaz, What day thou buyest the field of the hand of Naomi, thou must buy it also of Ruth the Moabitess, the wife of the dead, to raise up the name of the dead upon his inheritance.

6 And the kinsman said, I cannot redeem it for myself, lest I mar mine own inheritance: redeem thou my right to thyself; for I cannot redeem it.

7 Now this was the manner in former time in Israel concerning redeeming and concerning changing, for to confirm all things; a man plucked off his shoe, and gave it to his neighbour: and this was a testimony in Israel.

8 Therefore the kinsman said unto Boaz, Buy it for thee. So he drew off his shoe.

9 And Boaz said unto the elders, and unto all the people, Ye are witnesses this day, that I have bought all that was Elimelech's, and all that was Chilion's and Mahlon's, of the hand of Naomi.

10 Moreover Ruth the Moabitess, the wife of Mahlon, have I purchased to be my wife, to raise up the name of the dead upon his inheritance, that the name of the dead be not cut off from among his brethren, and from the gate of his place: ye are witnesses this day.

11 And all the people that were in the gate, and the elders, said, We are witnesses. The Lord make the woman that is come into thine house like Rachel and like Leah, which

two did build the house of Israel: and do thou worthily in Ephratah, and be famous in Bethlehem:

12 And let thy house be like the house of Pharez, whom Tamar bare unto Judah, of the seed which the Lord shall give thee of this young woman.

13 So Boaz took Ruth, and she was his wife: and when he went in unto her, the Lord gave her conception, and she bare a son.

14 And the women said unto Naomi, Blessed be the Lord, which hath not left thee this day without a kinsman, that his name may be famous in Israel.

15 And he shall be unto thee a restorer of thy life, and a nourisher of thine old age: for thy daughter in law, which loveth thee, which is better to thee than seven sons, hath born him.

16 And Naomi took the child, and laid it in her bosom, and became nurse unto it.

17 And the women her neighbours gave it a name, saying, There is a son born to Naomi; and they called his name Obed: he is the father of Jesse, the father of David.

18 Now these are the generations of Pharez: Pharez begat Hezron,

19 And Hezron begat Ram, and Ram begat Amminadab,

20 And Amminadab begat Nahshon, and Nahshon begat Salmon,

21 And Salmon begat Boaz, and Boaz begat Obed,

22 And Obed begat Jesse, and Jesse begat David.

FURTHER READING

- David Atkinson, *The Message of Ruth: The Wings of Refuge (The Bible Speaks Today Series)*, (Downers Grove, IL: IVP, 1983).
- Geoffrey T. Bull, *Love-Song in Harvest: An Interpretation of the Book of Ruth* (London: Pickering and Inglis, 1972).
- Stephen Dray, *Judges, and Ruth (Focus on the Bible)*, (Fearn, UK: Christian Focus Publications, 1997).
- Paul R. House, *Old Testament Theology* (especially chapter 18), (Downers Grove, IL: IVP Academic, 1998).
- Robert L. Hubbard, Jr., *The Book of Ruth (New International Commentary on the Old Testament)*, (Grand Rapids, MI: Eerdmans, 1988).
- Francine Rivers, *Unshaken (The Lineage of Grace #3)*, (Carol Stream, IL: Tyndale House Publishers, 2001).
- Warren W. Wiersbe, *Put Your Life Together: Studies*

in the Book of Ruth (Chicago, IL: Victor Books, 1985).

ACKNOWLEDGMENTS

Writing a brief "Acknowledgements" section is always the scariest part of completing a book. I worry that I will leave someone out. And then I wonder if I am giving the reader way more information than is needed. (Like those endless Christmas family updates that are never read.) But there are some people to be named and thanked.

I am thankful for a few friends who took the manuscript and read it in its early form. John Schoen and I were in an email exchange about the book and produced one of the longest email threads in my life. Thank you! Amber Gallaway is a great encourager. She helped me immensely in writing the questions at the end of each chapter. I have a few friends who read over a few chapters and said, "Keep going!" Bruce Barbour, John Wallace, John Tuthill, Greg Goebel, and my wife Fran were all a blessing to me in this way.

I wanted to ask some pretty ordinary people to read the book and give a note of encouragement. I invited a large group of people to self-identify as an "ordinary person" and then read the manuscript and write a short comment or blurb. They did! A lot of them! We published their names, words, blurbs, and endorsements in the following pages of the book. They are wonderfully "ordinary people" in the sense of the Book of Ruth—people whom our extraordinary God can use in ordinary ways to do beautiful things. I am thankful to all of them.

I also thank the Lord Jesus, the living Holy Spirit, and the loving Father in Heaven for the joy and privilege of reading God's Word. The Word of God is active, as it says. It is alive, as most readers will sense when they read Scripture. And it is endlessly amazing and rich with meaning, purpose, insight, and inspiration.

The Rev. Canon David H. Roseberry

www.LeaderWorks.org

www.DavidRoseberry.com

The Ordinary Way of God is an amazing book. I am not a quick reader, but it had me so captivated that I read it in a day. It gives an in-depth account of Ruth's story and a point of view that I had never seen in all the times of reading it. This book is a must-read for anyone, especially those who think that their choices are inconsequential to the bigger picture that God has planned.

— KIM NORRIS

Feeling ordinary? Feeling down? Feeling overwhelmed by the problems of everyday life? Then read The Ordinary Way of God. It will lift you up and bring you closer to the Lord. It did that for me!

— JOE FRANCIS

What a warm, delightful book about Ruth, this young woman of such remarkable strength and character! David drew me in with his contextual and spiritual insights, plus by crafting my favorite sentence from the richness of this significant and loved book.

— JO GRAY

David has a gift for bridging the centuries, bridging cultures, bridging genders. He makes Naomi and Ruth's time and place shine a light on each of our times and places. He walks us through the down-then-up journey God set out for them. A journey God knows will change the world.

— JOHN SCHOEN

What a remarkable and thought-provoking book—
The Ordinary Way of God by David Roseberry. I
have read the Book of Ruth several times and
listened to sermons about it, but this is the first
time I have truly understood what the Book of
Ruth is about. Roseberry takes a deep dive into
each chapter and reveals new insight into how God
uses ordinary people in extraordinary ways to
demonstrate His unending and unconditional love
for us. Lessons from this beautiful story can be
applied today. But it is so much more than a
beautiful story and much more profound than ever
imagined. The intricate work of the Holy Spirit is
woven throughout the story and well worth
reading.

— PATTI CLAAR

David Roseberry's book, written with such clarity and wisdom, has brought such comfort to my soul by assuring me that God is always present, despite how distant He may feel at times. Yearning for the "mountain top" experiences has been my desire, but now through this teaching, I have come to recognize God's glorious and mighty Hand hidden in the mundane moments of life. Each chapter is rich with lessons that illuminate the Holy Bible and its application today. As a result, I feel even more loved, protected, grateful, and at peace knowing the God of the ordinary by studying the Book of Ruth through the lens of such an anointed author.

— LINDA MULCHIN, R.N.

I knew Ruth's story, but this book expanded my understanding of her culture and God's ways of working in real people's lives. There are also practical applications for today and a clear picture of the Old and New Testaments' unity.

— ANN DELP

David Roseberry has the rare gift of guiding the reader through an inspiring devotional experience while at the same time providing the background information and context needed to understand Scripture. His overview of the Book of Ruth is concise but comprehensive, and his reflections on Ruth and her story are relevant and anything but ordinary!

— THE REV. GREG GOEBEL

The Ordinary Way of God is well written, flows smoothly, and captured my interest from Prologue to Epilogue. Explanations of key customs are significant to promote understanding the culture of the time. As a result of reading this book, I better appreciate ordinary people's role to impact extraordinary events such as being participants in the lineage of our Savior Jesus Christ.

— JANET CLARK

Roseberry's book on Ruth lights up the historical context, social mores, cultural and religious influences to illumine a richer and deeper story. This draws the reader to absorb the Book of Ruth's entirety, which reveals the relatable story about loss and grief and redemption. Read, mark, learn and inwardly digest this sumptuous meal about Naomi and Ruth's path to contentment under the divine guidance of God.

— SHARON FOX

Religious books are like church music—they usually either appeal to the heart or the head, but seldom both. David has achieved the near-impossible with this book. It appeals to both and is full of "aha!" insights. You'll gain an entirely new appreciation for Ruth and Naomi and their unique relationship and how God uses ordinary people in remarkable ways. You'll see clearly that God has a plan for each of us.

— THE REV. DALE CHRISMAN

This tour of the Book of Ruth opens many aspects of reflection and application for the Christian today. I highly recommend this book for a devotional, a retreat, or a home-group. Each chapter is brief and accessible and will occasion edifying spiritual conversations.

— THE REV. DR. DUANE MILLER

The Ordinary Way of God defines the often searched for, a relationship with God that many long for. I was mesmerized as he laid out this beautiful story of hope and redemption that he describes as the foreshadowing of what Christ does for all God's people. We all need the promise of being moved from despair to hope.

— ELAINE ABBOTT

David beautifully illuminates Ruth's story. Even though the mystery of God's presence isn't always self-evident in its silence, He's always there, blending into the ordinary fabric of our life, guiding us in ways that are often incomprehensible. This book provides awareness and appreciation for how God uses the most ordinary happenings of life to help shape our lives, even when he's furthest from our minds.

— THE REV. RANDY MELTON

Canon David has done it once again! While reading The Ordinary Way of God, I found myself thinking, "I have never thought of this before." After 40 years of ministry, I now have a much clearer understanding of the Book of Ruth and how the ministry of Jesus fulfilled many of the themes found in this timeless narrative. Canon David's description of how God uses ordinary people to fulfill God's purposes is inspiring. I have a greater appreciation of what God is doing around me and trusting Him rather than trying to control outcomes. I will order a copy of this book for every person in my parish. This book will benefit the seasoned minister as well as encourage parishioners and members of your community.

— THE REV. HAL SCOTT

This enlightening read dives into the Book of Ruth, emerging with a thought-provoking image of our amazing God, using ordinary people to accomplish His plan. Connections to our redemption and restoration are illuminated in this short but inclusive book! Inspirational for anyone desiring a closer relationship with our loving God.

— THE REV. SANDRA RIOS-DORIA

This book ministered to me! As a mother of four teens, my life can feel swallowed up in the ordinary. There are always things to clean, errands to run, and meals to cook! I struggle with whether what I do means anything. Thank you, David, for showing me through The Ordinary Way of God that God is always in the ordinary and that in our ordinary, everyday walk with God, He can do extraordinary things.

— ASHLEY WALLACE, AUTHOR OF "A THRILL OF HOPE."

I just finished reading The Ordinary Way of God, and I loved how Ruth's story was not only about redemption but also about how God uses ordinary people to accomplish His will, and that's good news!

— GAIL BERNARD

Ruth is my favorite book in the Bible. I have read and studied it numerous times. It wasn't until The Ordinary Way of God that I fully understood why. It is a beautiful story of ordinary people being used by God for His extraordinary purpose. This includes me.

— AMBER GALLAWAY

The Ordinary Way of God takes this seemingly ordinary story of family allegiance and digs deeper to show just how each action has a purpose and a reason. The story reflects Ruth's faith, which adds to Israel's people's history, eventually culminating in the Messiah's birth. Roseberry's book spans the Ordinary to the Extraordinary and everything in between.

— JENNIFER LOFGREN

With utter simplicity and an incredible knack for masterful use of the turn of a phrase, David Roseberry captures one of Scripture's most profound truths. This truth is hidden in plain sight. David's writing brings familiar passages alive, revealing the deep love and patience of a God who chooses to work through human beings. So often, we look for God to move in spectacular ways, missing the breathtaking God moments that occur in the ordinary events of life. If you are stuck in a Bible reading rut or need a fresh glimpse of God, this book is for you.

Pastor Becky Neumann

If you feel that God is not working in your life, this look at the often-overlooked Book of Ruth will reassure you that God is working even in difficult times, even when you don't hear God, even if you are an ordinary person leading an everyday life.

— VICTORIA SCHWARTZ

"Entreat Me Not to Leave Thee" are words from an anthem that I have sung at numerous weddings. The words come from the first chapter of the Book of Ruth. Ruth's words are spoken not to a husband but her mother-in-law. They talk of Ruth's devotion to Naomi and her later commitment to her husband, Boaz. David captures many of these gems in his book. As he says, this book was written for us—ordinary people. God is not mentioned or quoted, but the whole book is about God's Providence in our daily lives. I like the quote, "God uses our everyday efforts to accomplish His will" He goes on to say that we are free, but God is sovereign. That is a mystery.

— MERRITT FELMLY

Sometimes, when I hear stories of how God has worked large miracles in other's lives, I can't help asking, "Why hasn't God done this in my life?"

David clearly explains what is already revealed in the Bible. God usually takes ordinary people and their ordinary daily acts to weave His miracles. Most of God's miracles do not involve earthquakes, fires, winds, pillars of cloud/fire, or a dry land crossing through a sea. Instead, God's miracles are usually revealed as a gentle whisper.

While I should and did know this, David's book (with the curious-sounding title) again brought God's assurance to the forefront of my mind and spirit. A simple but profound read. You will not find complicated theological terminology, a lot of Greek, Latin, or Hebrew, just plain-speaking comprehensible English.

— GARY HUNZIKER

David Roseberry presents Scripture in a fresh, understandable, and, yes, even fun way! The Ordinary Way of God brings the Book of Ruth to life . . . and expertly interprets the truth of God's presence in and for us "ordinary" folks! I was sad to finish! I definitely will give it several closer, more in-depth readings!

— BARBARA CASSERLEIGH

David Roseberry beautifully unpacks the multiple, rich layers of Ruth's short book, revealing how God works in often unrecognized ways in everyday people's lives. In his effortless style, David expands awareness of God's ways and greater purpose, bringing hope and joy for the journey.

— DEBBIE FINN

The Ordinary Way of God shines a brilliant light on a treasure in God's Word—the Book of Ruth. Roseberry recounts the story of desperate women in extraordinarily challenging circumstances who witness the magnificent mercy of God. Inspiring and full of hope, this book unfolds God's plan of redemption for these two foreign women, foreshadowing His plan to redeem the world.

— CINDY TELISAK

With David's thoughtful and insightful guidance through this powerful and timeless story, we come to understand that God is always with us. Ruth's story gives us cause to re-examine our own day-to-day lives and to recognize God's presence and appreciate His guidance. Everyone can benefit from knowing the story of Ruth. It's timeless, and yet, it is still valid today. Thank you, David, for your expertise and guidance.

— LARRY EDGEMON

DAVID ROSEBERRY is an ordained Anglican priest and has been in ministry for nearly 40 years. He was founding Rector of Christ Church in Plano for over 30 years and now is the founding director of LeaderWorks, a non-profit ministry that serves churches and church leaders. He is a speaker, writer, teacher, and minister at large for the Anglican Church in North America. David Roseberry lives in Prosper with his wife, Fran.

The Ordinary Way of God is David's fifth book

BOOKS FOR CHURCHES AND CHURCH LEADERS

Giving Up: *How Giving to God Renews Hearts, Changes Minds, and. Empowers Ministry*
The Rector and the Vestry: *The Essential Guide for the Anglican Church*

BOOKS FOR ALL

When the Lord is My Shepherd: *Finding Hope in a Hard Time*

The Psalm on the Cross: *A Journey to the Heart of Jesus Through Psalm 22*